Carolyn Hall

THE SEWING MACHINE CRAFT BOOK

THE SEWING MACHINE CRAFT BOOK

CAROLYN HALL

A William & Shirley Sayles Book

VNR VAN NOSTRAND REINHOLD COMPANY
NEW YORK CINCINNATI TORONTO LONDON MELBOURNE

Copyright (c) 1980 by Litton Educational
Publishing, Inc.
Library of Congress Catalog Card Number 79- 11965
ISBN 0-442-29748-3

Printed in the United States of America

Published by Van Nostrand Reinhold Company
A division of Litton Educational Publishing, Inc.
135 West 50th Street, New York, NY 10020, U.S.A.

Van Nostrand Reinhold Limited
1410 Birchmount Road
Scarborough, Ontario M1P 2E7, Canada

Van Nostrand Reinhold Australia Pty. Ltd.
17 Queen Street
Mitcham, Victoria 3132, Australia

Van Nostrand Reinhold Company Limited
Molly Millars Lane
Wokingham, Berkshire, England

16 15 14 13 12 11 10 9 8 7 6 5 4 3 2 1

Library of Congress Cataloging in Publication Data

Hall, Carolyn Vosburg, 1927-
  The sewing machine craft book.

  "A William & Shirley Sayles book."
  Includes index.
  1. Machine sewing. 2. Textile crafts. I. Title.
TT713.H33   746.4   79-11965
ISBN 0-442-29748-3

TABLE OF CONTENTS

ACKNOWLEDGMENTS

In the course of preparing this book, many fiber artists were asked for photographic examples of their work, and their cooperation was very gratifying. Thanks go to them and also to Mary Zdrodowsky who contributed suggestions for lettering styles.

INTRODUCTION

Say "sewing machine" to some people and they visualize a utilitarian tool busily stitching its way through mile after mile of fabric. But an increasing number of stitchers view the sewing machine quite differently — to them it is a means of achieving creative results quickly.

This book is for beginners, the newly initiated, and those who have been sewing "forever." It is divided into sections, each devoted to a different subject: there is information on the basics of sewing; on fabrics, how to buy them and prepare them for sewing; on threads, both traditional and unorthodox, how to use them in the machine or couch them on the fabric; and on the machine itself, its parts and accessories. Within the sections on sewing techniques are projects (complete with diagrams) that you can do, as well as design ideas that you can follow. Vary the projects, if you wish, or use them as starting points for your own ideas; experiment with them, using either one technique alone or in conjunction with another.

You can begin by making objects at once — a pillow, a purse, a stuffed figure — using any of the numerous techniques given: from embroidery and patchwork, appliqué and several quilting techniques, to cutwork, soft sculpture, and upholstery. This book also tells you how to coil a basket (on the machine), stitch flossa pile, make Seminole Indian designs, and stuff a wall hanging as you stitch it. Most of the objects can be made on ordinary sewing machines using fairly simple sewing techniques. The machine is only the technical tool, the take-off point. The most important ingredient is you — and your imagination—so it does not matter too much what kind of sewing machine you have—from old treadle to new superstar special. It is what you do with it that counts.

Photographs throughout the book illustrate various approaches to design and show some of the ways innovative textile artists have liberated the sewing machine to make all types of objects.

A number of artists are responsible for the current burst of excitement for machine-sewn art. Claes Oldenburg, an imaginative and versatile American artist, ranks high among them. His soft sculpture was first created in the 1960s, concurrent with the pop art trend—the icebag, the hamburger, and the piece of cake celebrated the ordinary in much the same way as did Andy Warhol's Campbell soup cans. Norman LaLiberté updated tapestries when he assembled colorful scraps of fabric into lively banners and wall hangings. Other textile artists, represented here and in galleries and craft museums throughout the country, are testimony to the exciting fact that the sewing machine, as the creative stitchers' tool, has arrived.

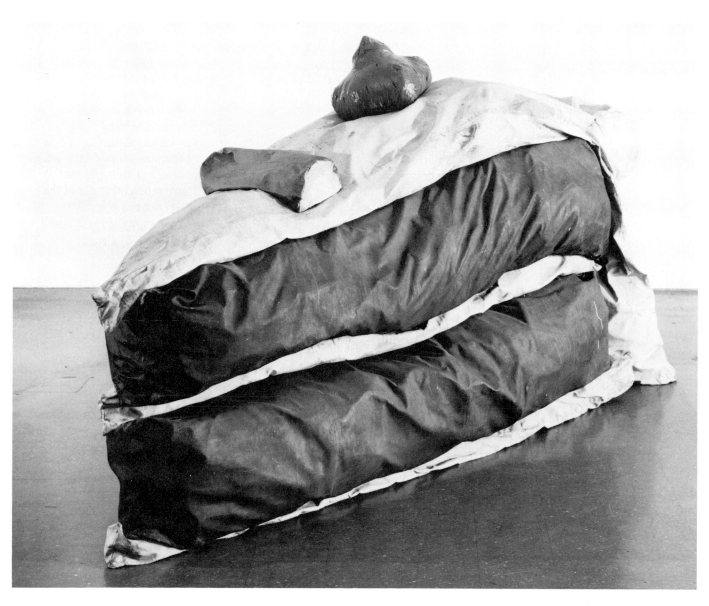

Floor Cake (Giant Piece of Cake)
by Claes Oldenburg (60″×9′×48″) 1962.
Synthetic polymer paint and latex on
canvas, filled with foam rubber. (Collection, The Museum of Modern Art, New
York. Gift of Philip Johnson)

1. THE SEWING MACHINE

The idea of a machine that would sew goes back to the middle of the eighteenth century when a German inventor patented one that required two complete passes through the fabric to make one stitch.

It took another ninety years of thought, work, trials, failures, and partial successes by many would-be inventors before Elias Howe patented the first workable sewing machine in 1846. This machine had a needle with its eye near the point to carry the top thread and a shuttle to carry a second thread. Although today's sewing machines differ greatly in appearance from that first model, the construction of the lockstitch remains the same.

Types of Machine. There are many makes and models of sewing machines, but the basic choice is between two types—the straight stitch or the zigzag. The straight stitch machine sews forward and (usually) in reverse and has an adjustable stitch length. A great variety of attachments is available to add versatility to this machine.

Versatility is built into the zigzag machine. Its swing needle moves from side to side as well as forward and in reverse, forming a line of zigzag stitches of different widths and lengths. The most advanced machines have interchangeable stitch patterns, making it possible to produce automatic decorative stitches just by flicking a knob or touching a button. (As a rule, textile artists are not very interested in programmed stitches, preferring to create their own designs.)

On some sewing machines, the conventional flatbed sewing surface can be converted to a free arm. This armlike extension of the main body is open all around and is extremely helpful for sewing curved seams and tubular shapes.

To get the most enjoyment and efficiency from your machine, learn how to operate and care for it right from the start. Read your machine manual carefully and keep it handy. This indispensable booklet describes the workings of your particular machine.

The information in this section will help you select a machine if you do not already own one, or realize the potential of the one you do own.

Figure 1-1. Sewing machine prototype.

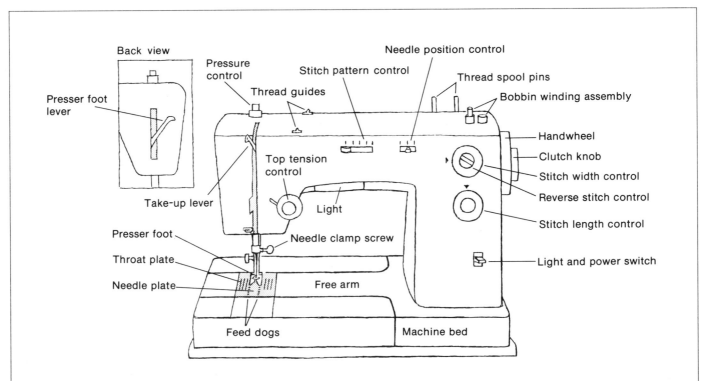

PARTS OF THE MACHINE

The machine prototype shown in Figure 1-1 may be different from your machine in the placement of its operating parts, but the parts themselves are common to most machines.

Spool Pin—holds spools of various sizes. Some machines have two spool pins for twin-needle sewing or for allowing a bobbin to be wound without disturbing the threading on the machine.

Top Tension Control—consists of discs between which the top thread passes and a dial control which increases or decreases pressure on the thread as it feeds through the machine. The higher the number dialed, the tighter the tension. When tension on the top and bottom threads is equal, the result is a balanced stitch.

Take-up Lever—controls the flow of the top thread. It has an eyelet or slot through which the thread passes.

Pressure Control—controls the amount of pressure the presser foot exerts on the fabric.

Presser Foot—holds fabric in place for stitching. Different types of presser feet are available.

Presser Foot Lever—raises and lowers the presser foot. Tension discs are engaged when the foot is down; there is no tension when the foot is up. In the up position, thread can be easily pulled to begin or end stitching.

Feed Dogs—move fabric into position for each stitch. They can be disengaged for certain sewing techniques by setting the feed control to the down position.

Needle Plate—has slots for the feed and a hole for the needle. There are two types: straight stitch (small needle hole) and zigzag stitch (wide needle hole). The zigzag plate, also called multi-purpose, accommodates all types of stitching; the straight stitch plate may be needed for close control or delicate fabrics, for example.

Stitch Length Control—regulates the length of each stitch. The control is numbered in stitches per inch (the higher the number, the shorter the stitch) or measured in millimeters (the lower the number, the shorter the stitch).

Stitch Width Control—regulates the width, or bight, of the zigzag stitch. The higher the number, the wider the stitch.

Stitch Pattern Control—allows for a quick selection of built-in decorative stitches; it includes diagrams of various patterns. On some machines, cams are inserted to produce the stitches.

Handwheel—commonly used to raise the bobbin thread when sewing begins. It may also be used to start or stop the machine when very fine control is needed, especially if the foot pedal is not very sensitive and the machine "runs on."

Clutch Knob (or flywheel)—located in the center of the handwheel. On some machines, the knob has to be loosened during bobbin winding to stop the up and down action of the needle.

Bobbin—flat, wide metal or clear plastic spool which holds the bobbin thread (some older machines have long, skinny spools). Use the type recommended for your machine, and buy at least a dozen.

Bobbin Winder—holds the bobbin during winding. Depending on the model, the bobbin-winding mechanism can be outside (at the top or side) or inside the machine. On some machines, a latch or pressure guide controls threading and shuts off automatically when the bobbin is full.

Bobbin Case—holds the bobbin in place. A tension spring or latch controls the flow of thread. Buy an extra bobbin case for experimental stitching.

Shuttle—a hollow ring, located under the needle and throat plate, into which the bobbin case is fitted and locked in place.

Needle Position Control—moves the needle to the left or right of its normally center position. This is helpful in making buttonholes and in positioning special stitches.

Figure 1-2. Bobbin assembly. Vertically mounted removable bobbin case. Contains threaded bobbin.

SEWING MACHINE ACCESSORIES

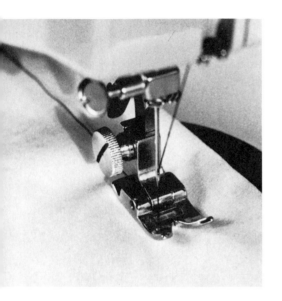

Figure 1-3. Zigzag presser foot in action.

Presser Feet

Various types of presser feet are available to increase the stitch versatility of the sewing machine and to help speed certain tasks. Most are made of metal to provide a smooth and durable surface. Some are Teflon-coated; others are clear plastic for greater stitch visibility (especially helpful in embroidery). A few are hinged to facilitate sewing over pins and bulky seams.

Each machine requires a particular type of shank (length and angle of upper part of presser foot): long shank, short shank, or slant needle shank. When buying a presser foot, be sure it will fit your machine. To be certain, take a presser foot from your machine with you or consult your manual.

A representative selection of presser feet follows. You may find that you never need to use many of the ones described here, but at least you will know what is available. The most essential arc thc first four listed. Throughout this book various presser feet are suggested, just in case you have them on hand or want to experiment, but, in actuality, I almost never change presser feet. Unless I need some special quality, the zigzag foot is suitable for all my work.

Straight Stitch Foot—narrow, with a small hole for single-needle straight stitching. It is especially used to hold sheer fabrics firmly.

Zigzag Foot (also called all-purpose foot)—has a wide hole for zigzag stitching. It can be used for straight stitching as well.

Darning Foot—an enclosed shape with a wide hole. It permits close control of both stitch and fabric. It is recommended for embroidery, especially free motion embroidery, and can also be used for quilting. Some machines use a darning spring instead of a foot.

Special-Purpose Foot (also called embroidery foot)— grooved on the bottom to allow easy movement over raised stitches, especially satin stitches.

Adjustable Zipper Foot—permits stitching close to an edge that is more raised on one side than the other,

Figure 1-4 A and B. Presser feet.

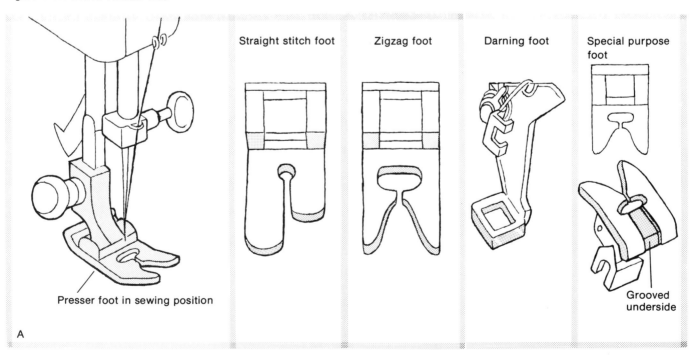

Presser foot in sewing position

A

Straight stitch foot

Zigzag foot

Darning foot

Special purpose foot

Grooved underside

such as a zipper or cording. It can be moved to the right or left of the needle. It is recommended for quilting.

Button Foot—holds buttons in place during stitching. You can also use a zigzag foot if, at the start, you hold the button with your fingers and turn the handwheel manually.

Overcast Foot—built-in guide keeps stitches from drawing tightly and puckering a zigzag overcast edge. This foot can also be used to make tailor tacks.

Narrow Hemmer—turns a rolled hem and stitches it in place.

Even Feed Foot—helps both layers of fabric to feed evenly. Used for hard-to-feed fabrics, such as velvet and jersey. Instead of this foot, you can tape seams, pin baste, hand baste, or ease pressure on the presser foot.

Roller Foot—another top feed assist; it serves the same purpose as the even feed. Both feet work best when stitching long, straight seams; they are too clumsy for intricate stitching.

Figure 1-5. Free motion pattern in straight stitch.

Figure 1-6. Detail of framed stitchery by Carlos Cobos. Appliquéd ribbons with satin stitching along all edges.

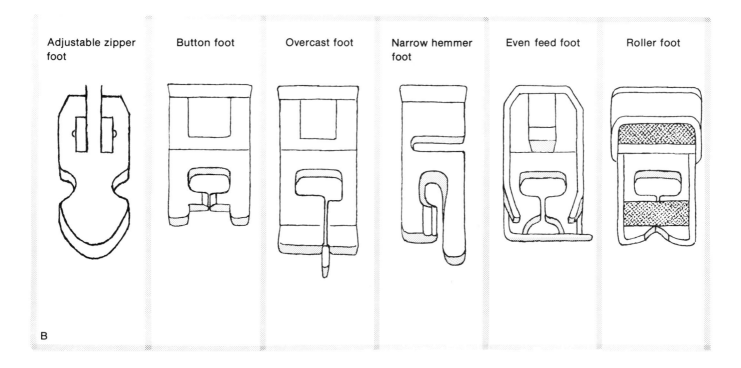

| Adjustable zipper foot | Button foot | Overcast foot | Narrow hemmer foot | Even feed foot | Roller foot |

B

Needles

The upper part of a sewing machine needle, called the body, is rounded on one side and flat on the other side. The flat side helps you to insert the needle correctly. The lower, thinner part is called the shaft. Extending along the shaft, from the rounded portion of the body and down to the eye, is a groove that guides the thread as it feeds. Above the eye, on the flat side of the needle, is the scarf; its notched shape allows the needle to clear the shuttle. The eye is just above the needle point.

Needles come in different sizes and types to suit various stitching requirements. No matter what size or type needle you select, be sure it matches the make and model number of your machine. A mismatched needle, as well as one that is dull, bent, nicked, or improperly inserted, will pucker threads, cause skipped stitches, or mark delicate fabrics. Before beginning a project, test the needle on a piece of scrap fabric; if it is dull or bent, discard and replace it. Needles dull quickly, especially when used with synthetics.

Sizes. Match needle size to thread weight. The higher the number, the thicker the needle. By buying the smallest size needle that will accommodate a given thread, you can prevent damage to the fabric (important in knits) or large holes (important in non-woven or pressed fabrics). If the thread frays or breaks, change to a needle in the next largest size. Keep a supply of various sizes on hand. European needles are also available and will probably fit your machine.

The chart that follows gives American needle sizes in a range from 9 (finest) to 18 (coarsest), together with equivalent European sizes.

Figure 1-7. Sewing machine needle (front and back views).
Different needle points.
Other needle types.

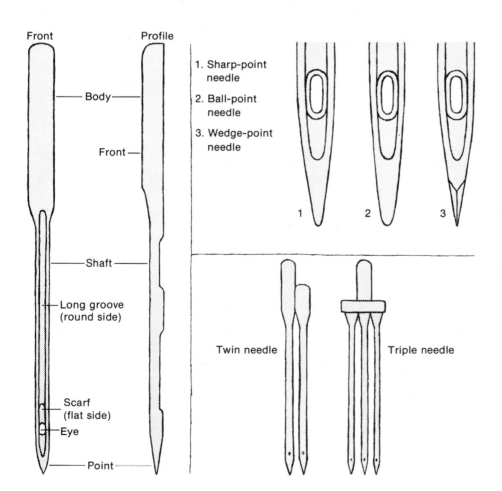

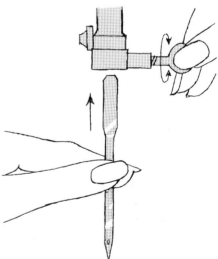

Figure 1-8. Inserting needle. Loosen screw, insert needle all the way up into clamp, tighten screw.

Needle Sizes

American	European
9	60
-	70
11	-
-	80
14	90
16	100
18	110
-	120

Types. Different needle points are designed for use with different fabrics. The *sharp-point (regular) needle,* the one most often used, is suitable for all types of woven fabrics. The *ball-point* needle is recommended for knits and synthetics. Its rounded point slips gently between the cloth fibers (unlike the sharp-point needle which pierces the fibers), thus preventing skipped stitches and damage to fabrics. A *wedge-point needle* cuts knifelike through non-porous fabrics, such as leather and vinyl, making a hole that closes upon itself.

Some needles are used mainly for decorative stitching and only with zigzag machines. A *twin needle* stitches parallel lines of straight, zigzag, or pattern stitches; a *triple needle* is also available. Using two (or more) threads of different colors and/or textures in these needles can enhance stitch patterns. Stitches are formed in the same way as with a single needle, except that there are two (or three) top threads for the bobbin hook to catch instead of one. Check your manual to see if these needles can be used in your machine.

Figure 1-9. The sharp-point needle *(top)* pierces the threads of knits and synthetics. The ball-point needle *(bottom)* gently separates the threads and slips between them.

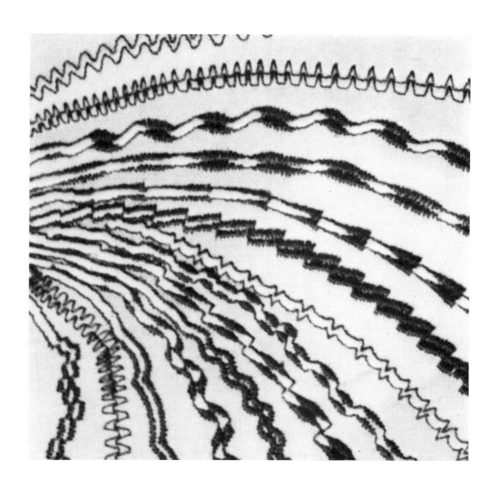

Figure 1-10. Automatic stitches made with twin needles. (Courtesy, Yvanne Ham)

BUYING A MACHINE

Many factors influence the purchase of a machine, not the least of which is cost, so it pays to watch for sales which occur periodically in this competitive field. As a rule, the more a machine can do, the more expensive it will be. Machines are similar in basic features, but differ in performance, simplicity of use, weight, and special features. Ideally you should know what you want a machine to do and can select one on that basis, but, in reality, most creative people have little idea of what they will be trying next, so a versatile machine may be the wisest choice.

The best way to select a machine is to visit the sewing centers maintained by the various manufacturers and try out the machines under the supervision of a trained salesperson. Take your own fabric samples with you since the "test" fabrics used at the sewing centers are stiffened and never pucker. Another way to try out a machine is to rent before buying or to ask for a home trial; some companies provide these services. Some also provide free lessons when you purchase a new machine. Do take the lessons to learn the capabilities of your machine and the latest in sewing techniques. Buying from a good dealer is also important for both service and advice, so take this into consideration when shopping around.

When trying out a machine, look for these points:
- An easily adjustable, plainly marked top thread tension control.
- Ease of threading, bobbin winding, and needle changing.
- Easy access to the bobbin area.
- Feed dogs that can be dropped or covered.
- Presser foot pressure control.
- A convenient foot or knee control.
- Zigzag settings for versatility.

Some machines have two speeds: fast for normal sewing and slow for detailed work or heavy fabrics.

Used Machines. For a dependable used machine, it is best to buy from a reputable dealer. The dealer will insure that the machine is in satisfactory condition before issuing a service warranty. Buying from other sources, such as want ads, involves

Figure 1-11. *Our Neighbors Across the Alley* by Dee Durkee (34½"×21"×2"). Window hanging. Stitched and stuffed canvas; painted with acrylics and ink.

some risk, so you must check out the machine carefully. The same convenience factors you would look for in a new machine apply to a used one as well. But also make sure the machine can stitch a perfectly straight seam, that its light is well-positioned, and that wiring is in good condition. Consider other factors as well. How much will the machine do without added attachments? Are all necessary attachments and parts available? Is service convenient to where you live? And, finally, does an instruction manual come with the machine?

MAINTENANCE

Sewing machines, properly used and cared for, will give a lifetime of service. For example, many of the old, picturesque treadle machines are still in service and are being put to vigorous use. These machines can be used to make many of the projects in this book, although, of course, newer machines do the work faster and more easily.

To insure the best possible results from your machine, and to save on repair bills, you must keep its moving parts clean. When you sew, the fabric leaves lint deposits that accumulate around the bobbin case and feed dogs. Before each project (or at least periodically) remove the needle and throat plates and brush away this lint with a small brush. Also, wipe the surfaces of the machine with a clean cloth or wash gently with a sponge. Cover the machine when it is not in use.

A periodic oiling keeps the machine running freely. If you cannot remember the last time you oiled the machine, it is probably time to do it again. Refer to your manual for the points to oil. Mark these points with nail polish so you will not have to refer to the manual each time. Be careful not to get polish on working parts. Only use oil made specifically for sewing machines. After oiling the machine, run it slowly for several minutes to allow the oil to penetrate. Keep a small piece of fabric under the presser foot to absorb any excess.

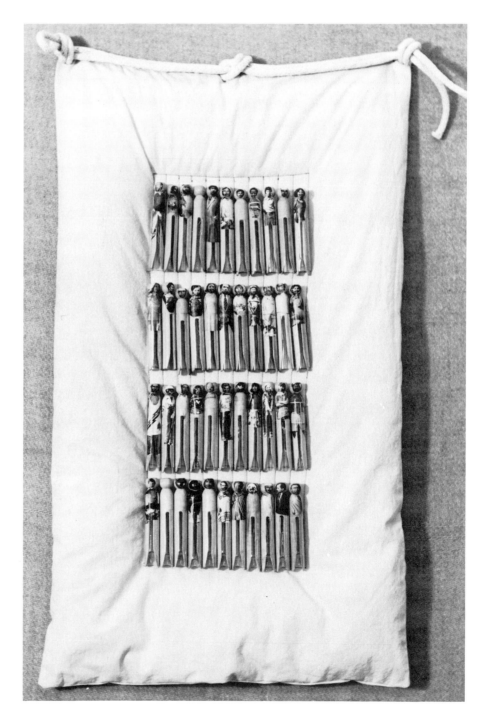

Figure 1-12. *Census* by Carolyn Hall (36" × 20" × 1"). Stuffed backing provides frame; clear vinyl strips stitched to backing make slots for clothespins decorated with glued on magazine cutouts. (Collection, Dr. William Squires)

COMMON PROBLEMS

Most stitching problems are not serious, and in most cases, you will quickly solve them yourself. Often they can be traced to improper threading; a bent, blunt, or incorrectly inserted needle; the wrong size needle or thread; tension that is too tight or too loose; or thread and/or lint caught in the shuttle. The problems caused by these and other factors are listed below. Any irregularities that you cannot remedy should be checked by your repair service.

Needle Thread Breaks
- Machine improperly threaded.
- Needle bent or blunt or has a burr.
- Needle incorrectly inserted.
- Thread old and brittle.
- Knot in thread.
- Top tension too tight.
- Needle plate nicked.

Bobbin Thread Breaks
- Bobbin case improperly threaded.
- Bobbin case improperly inserted.
- Bobbin thread unevenly wound.
- Bobbin tension too tight.
- Lint in bobbin case or shuttle.

Needle Breaks
- Wrong size needle.
- Bent needle.
- Needle incorrectly inserted.
- Loose presser foot.
- Fabric being pulled while sewing.

Thread Bunches
- Not drawn under presser foot.
- Feed is down.
- Presser foot lever not lowered.

Figure 1-13. *Free Spirit* by Cindy Hickok (each figure approximately 48″ × 18″). Quilted to delineate features and sayings. (Collection, Rodrigo Trejos)

Fabric Puckers
- Fabric too sheer or too soft.
- Thread too heavy.
- Tensions too tight.
- Stitches too long or too short.
- Presser foot pressure too light or too heavy.

Uneven Stitches
- Fabric being pulled while sewing.
- Wrong size needle.
- Improper threading.
- Tensions too loose.

Stitches Skip
- Wrong size or type needle.
- Bent or blunt needle.
- Needle incorrectly inserted.
- Needle not all the way up in clamp.
- Presser foot pressure too light.
- Stitches too near edge of fabric.

Machine Jams
- Thread caught in shuttle.
- Lint in shuttle.

Machine is Sluggish
- Needs cleaning and/or oiling.

WORK SPACE

In order to work most effectively, you need to organize an area for your sewing machine and other sewing necessities. A separate sewing room is ideal, of course, but a corner in a room or space near a window can be a satisfactory and comfortable arrangement. With good planning, and at little expense, you can avoid the hassle of pulling the sewing machine out of hiding, looking for fabric stashed here and there, and, all in all, spending as much time assembling your equipment as it takes to do the project you have planned.

Whether you have a lot of room or need to make every inch of space count, your basic requirements remain the same:

Good Lighting—consider an adjustable lamp that clamps to your work table and spotlights the work area.

A Sturdy Table (or console)—on which to place the sewing machine. Be sure that it is at the proper height for comfort.

A Large Table—for cutting (or use the floor).

A Comfortable Chair or Stool—the right height for you.

Pressing Equipment—keep nearby.

Storage For Small Items—many aids are available: bobbin holders, spool holders, and sewing chests of various sizes and types. A pegboard mounted on a wall or inside a closet door will hold most measuring equipment and sewing accessories (not scissors—keep these in a drawer). A spice rack is another space stretcher. Bulky or oddly shaped items can be stored in plastic bins, straw baskets, or shoe boxes, all of uniform size for stacking.

Storage for Large Items—cabinets, shelves, and storage boxes or baskets will keep projects and fabrics clean and out of the way until needed.

Creative stitchers need a large collection of materials on hand to inspire them—velvets may not be available in the summer, or some cottons in the fall. Sort fabrics in a way most useful to you—by color for instance.

Figure 1-14. *Three Dolls* by Robin Haarer (each 16″ tall). Machine-sewn figures made of a variety of fabrics; stitching and painting in areas.

2. TOOLS AND MATERIALS

FOR MEASURING

Most measuring devices are marked in centimeters as well as in inches. Be careful not to interchange measurements.

Sewing Gauge—6-inch (15.2 cm) metal ruler with a sliding marker.

Tape Measure—60-inch (152 cm) length, marked on both sides. Select one with a metal tip on each end and made of material that will not stretch or tear.

Transparent Ruler—available in a variety of shapes and sizes.

Yardstick—useful for taking long, straight measurements and for checking grainlines.

French Curve—can be used to mark straight lines as well as curves. It has a marking guide for 5/8 inch (1.6 cm) seam allowances.

FOR CUTTING

Scissors and Shears

No matter what kind of cutting job you have, be assured there is a pair of scissors or shears designed to suit that purpose. Scissors and shears are not the same. Scissors are shorter, have ring handles of equal size, and are used for lighter jobs than shears. Shears have longer blades and contoured handles for more comfort and better leverage in cutting. Both come in many types and sizes including left-handed models.

Test several pairs before you buy. Find a pair in a size that feels comfortable in your hand. Open and close them a few times; they should work easily and smoothly, yet with a slight pressure. Try them out on different fabrics to see if the blades and points are sharp. The cut should be complete, from near the back of the blades to the tips, and the fabric should be released immediately. Buy only the best quality. Make sure that the blades are joined by a screw or bolt and not by a rivet. When riveted blades loosen, they cannot be tightened. With care, fine scissors and shears will last indefinitely. Use them only for fabric and have them sharpened by a professional at the first sign of dullness.

The scissors and shears listed here are the ones that you will find most helpful.

Bent Trimmers or Dressmaker Shears—have a bent handle that is angled to allow fabric to lie flat while being cut.

Light Trimmers—a good choice for trimming and clipping seams.

Sewing Scissors—for small jobs, such as trimming fabric and cutting

Figure 2-1. Measuring a sketch for accuracy.

Figure 2-2. Scissors and shears.

Bent trimmers

Light trimmers

Lingerie shears

Sewing scissors

Embroidery scissors

thread. One blade is pointed while the other is blunt.

Lingerie Shears—have long narrow blades for cutting sheer fabric and trimming close to the stitching line; one blade is serrated to keep fabric from slipping or stretching. A finger guide helps control the cutting.

Embroidery Scissors—have slender blades with needle-sharp points for intricate work.

Clippers—for small jobs, such as clipping threads and ripping out seams. Spring action instantly reopens the blades (sharp- or blunt-pointed) after each snip.

Electric Scissors—ease tired hands when there is a lot of cutting to do. They come either with a cord or cordless (battery-operated).

Other Cutting Tools

Seam Ripper—has a curved, sharp-bladed edge for taking out seams and removing stitches. This tool is a must. Choose one with a plastic safety ball.

Razor Blade or Mat Knife—can be used, with a ruler as a guide, for straight line cuts.

FOR PINNING

"See a pin and pick it up. All the day you'll have good luck," promises the old saying. Until about 150 years ago, when a machine was invented to cut and shape pins from a single piece of wire, rapidly making thousands, pins were uncommon and valuable. Pin cushions, simple or elegant, filled with sand or emery (for polishing rust from iron pins or tarnish from brass pins), were valued possessions.

Today, straight pins are available in several lengths and thicknesses to suit different fabrics: long pins for heavy fabrics, shorter pins for medium weight and fine fabrics.

Generally, the longer the pin, the thicker it is. It is difficult to push long (thick) pins through some synthetics, and they would make holes in fine fabrics. Short (thin) pins bend when pushed through heavy fabrics. Pins come with flat metal heads or with glass or plastic color ball heads; the latter are more practical since they are easier to see and handle. Dressmaker or silk pins are nonrusting and will not mark fine fabrics; use only the finest and the sharpest. Ball-point pins are rounded and, therefore, good for knits.

Pins are available in paper packets or in plastic boxes. Buying them in one-pound packages is most economical. They may also be specially ordered in larger quantities. Together with the pins, you will want a pin-cushion. Also you will find a magnet very handy for picking up pins and needles gone astray on the floor or in the rug.

Figure 2-3. Cutting tools.

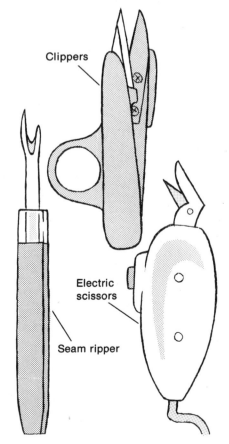

Clippers

Electric scissors

Seam ripper

Figure 2-4. Pinning fabric strips in place for stitching.

FOR PRESSING

There is a difference between ironing and pressing. Ironing is a sliding motion, with pressure over the entire surface, whereas pressing is a repeated gentle, up and down motion in a concentrated area, with steam doing the work. Steam can be generated by pressing on a dampened cloth or by using a steam iron.

A good iron is a necessity, primarily for pressing seams flat for the next sewing step. If you are planning to buy a new iron, visit a store that carries several brands and do some comparison shopping. A combination steam-and-dry iron with a wide temperature range is the most practical to own. It should be lightweight, balance well in your hand, and remain in position when stood on its heel rest (since the iron will be on a padded ironing board, it could easily keel over if not stable). See if the temperature control is easy to operate, and, if you are left-handed, whether the cord is convertible. Also see if the iron has a Teflon-coated soleplate. This coating resists starch, sizing, and lint buildup; it scratches more easily than an uncoated plate, but its performance is not affected. Finally, find out if the iron can be easily cleaned. Ideally, distilled water should be used in steam irons, but some have self-cleaning features to prevent clogging from tap water mineral deposits.

In addition to the iron, you will need a sturdy and adjustable ironing board. Keep it well padded. To press shaped seams, a firmly stuffed cushion called a tailor's ham comes in handy as does a press cloth; the latter protects fabric from direct contact with the hot iron and prevents iron shine and press marks.

Other pressing aids can be added if and when needed, but most will not be necessary for designer-stitchers.

Figure 2-5. Pressing equipment.

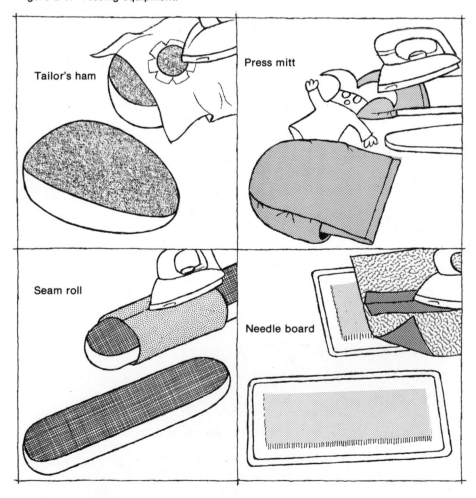

Tailor's ham

Press mitt

Seam roll

Needle board

Figure 2-6. *Cat Quilt* by Carolyn Hall (77"
× 48"). Machine-stitched cotton suede
and velvet quilt. Photograph of cat, screen
printed and dye painted.

THREADS

The invention of the sewing machine created a new industry—the manufacture of strong, supple thread of uniform sizes. Since the top thread goes forward and back through the eye of the needle thirty to ninety times (and sometimes more) before it is incorporated into a stitch, it has to be strong. Poor quality thread can jam your machine and cause other problems.

Choose thread that is compatible with the weight of the fabric and suited to the work at hand. Thread, on the whole, should be also be in harmony with the fiber content of the fabric; synthetic thread for synthetic fabric, fine thread for sheer fabric, and heavy thread for heavy fabric (including leather and vinyl).

Needle size should always be the finest possible to accommodate the thread you have chosen. For pieces you plan to wash, choose threads that are also washable. If you want

stitches to be as invisible as possible, use a color slightly darker than the fabric (thread sews in lighter than it appears on the spool) or use clear nylon thread.

Some sewing threads are designated by numbers (the higher the number, the finer the thread), while others are designated by type.

Cotton thread comes in several sizes. The most common are 40 (heavy-duty, coarse), 50 (medium), and 60 (extra-fine). Size 50, an all-purpose thread, is available in a great variety of colors. Threads are often treated with finishes to lend them special qualities and to improve performance. The mercerization of cotton is such a process. It improves the strength and smoothness of the thread, reduces shrinkage, provides luster, and increases the absorbency of dyes. Both mercerized and untreated cotton thread can be bought economically on spools or cones at upholstery-supply stores or wholesale thread outlets. The colors of the untreated cotton may not be as bright and lustrous as those of the mercerized, but the cost is less.

Synthetic threads include clear nylon, polyester, and cotton-wrapped polyester. These are available in sizes comparable to 40, 50, and 60. Clear nylon thread has strength and a high elasticity. It can be used in the couching technique when you want nearly invisible stitches or on a fabric whose color you cannot match. This thread is stiff, so watch that it does not unwind or tangle as you use it. Polyester thread is suitable for most fabrics. Cotton-wrapped polyester, as its name explains, is a polyester thread wrapped with cotton. The cotton sheath provides heat resistance and makes the thread sew and appear like cotton, while the polyester core provides strength and elasticity. Threads that have elastic properties help keep seams from puckering, and they stretch with the fabric when stress is applied.

Figure 2-7. *Cat Pillow* by Mary Ellis (20″ × 24″ × 4″). An example of threads used to construct and delineate features of a form.

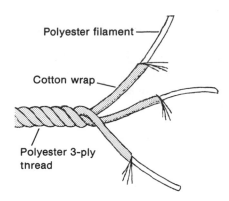

Polyester filament

Cotton wrap

Polyester 3-ply thread

Figure 2-8. Cotton-wrapped polyester thread; comparable to size 50 thread.

Most synthetic threads have a wax or silicone finish that helps them slide easily through a fabric. This quality is also achieved by glazing, a process used primarily on button and carpet thread, and on thread for hand and machine quilting. It gives a tough, smoothly polished surface.

Still other threads can be used in the machine: silk, a fine size (A) thread, is strong and has elasticity, making it a good choice for almost any fabric; buttonhole twist, an extra heavy silk thread, is suitable for decorative stitching and topstitching; embroidery floss, a 6-stranded thread, can be separated for fine work; and any decorative thread or yarn or string that can be threaded through the machine or wound onto the bobbin. Threads used in the bobbin can be thicker than those used in the needle. Using threads and yarns of different sizes and characteristics will usually require tension

adjustments. Those yarns or threads too heavy or fragile to pass through the machine or the fabric may be couched (laid on the fabric and stitched in place).

For smooth, fine-textured embroidery, the special left-twist machine embroidery cotton threads are best. They have a lovely sheen and are softer and more flexible than

regular sewing threads. Machine darning thread has properties similar to those of embroidery thread, but is less bulky and less expensive. It is ideal for use as the bobbin thread in embroidery. European embroidery threads are also available. Experiment with an assortment of different threads; new ones are being introduced all the time.

Figure 2-9. Detail of *Iris* by Edith Pirtle. A variety of fine threads on denim.

Figure 2-10. Detail of *Genesis* by Janet Kuemmerlein. Rich selection of yarns, loose and braided, couched to completely cover fabric background.

FABRICS

The colors, textures, strengths, and functions of fabric are as limitless as the list of their uses. We are surrounded by fabrics: we cover our walls and windows with them, we walk on them, sit on them, wear them. They provide us with necessities as well as with such wondrous things as hot air balloons and space suits. For the artist-stitchers, they are the raw materials for their inventions.

The way a fabric folds or drapes, stretches or gathers, reflects or absorbs light, can become an instrument for inspiration, influencing how the individual piece will be made and how it will look. Over the years, certain fabrics have developed reputations: velvet for luxury, denim for play, calico for nostalgia, lace for romance, wool for warmth. You can use these images in your work, or intentionally contradict them.

Learn all you can about fabric by experimenting with different kinds. Nothing quite compares with handling materials yourself to see what they can do. The one characteristic that all stitchers share is their love of fabrics. They cannot resist touching them; they know that a beautiful fabric gives tactile as well as visual pleasure.

Each fabric (natural and synthetic) has its particular strengths and weaknesses, its unique characteristics of resiliency, softness, and luster. The right fabric can "make" the piece. So it will be worth your while to spend time in different fabric stores getting to know the many types available. Some stores specialize in designer fabrics; some in practical fabrics of good quality and washability; still others in seconds, mill ends, and remnants.

A tour of a fabric store will show fabrics in a seemingly endless variety of choices: sheer or heavy, soft or stiff, stretchy or stable, fluid or firm, plain or fancy, printed or embossed.

Most fabrics are either woven or knitted, with weaving the more frequently used method. Other methods of making fabric include felting (perhaps the oldest way), netting, and braiding, and the newer processes of fusing, bonding, and laminating, in which adhesives interlock short fibers or glue fabrics together.

Woven fabrics are produced by interlacing lengthwise yarns (the warp) with crosswise yarns (the weft, or filling). Most weaves are variations on three basic weaves: plain, twill, and satin. The simplest and most commonly used is the plain weave, also called tabby. We come upon this weave everyday in percales, muslins, ginghams, chambrays, chiffons, organdies, chintzes, crepes, and shantungs. Twill weave produces diagonal ridges on the face of the fabric. Examples are gabardine and denim. Pile weave, a variation on plain or twill, is woven of three sets of yarns with the third set drawn into loops on the fabric surface. The loops can be cut, sheared, or left in loop form. Examples are corduroy, velour, velvet, velveteen, plush, terry cloth, and fake fur (which can also be knitted). In satin weave, the warp yarn passes over four or more weft yarns, leaving floats (exposed yarns) on the surface. These floats produce the smooth sheen associated with satin.

Knitted fabrics are made up of a series of interlocking loops that result in a flexible construction. Plain knit jersey and double knits are chief examples of the many fabrics produced by this technique.

Various finishes given to fabrics add texture and design, and otherwise alter appearance and performance. One example is napping (surfaces are brushed to create a soft, downy texture, as in flannel), an-other is flocking (fibers are applied to an adhesive surface, as in suede cloth—which can also be woven or knitted).

Using Fabric

Any fabric that can be stitched through your machine is worth investigating and using for experimentation. That includes leather, the leather-look vinyls, suede (both real and fake), as well as plastic, metallic, and glass fabrics. As you experiment, you will discover how different fabrics respond to different techniques.

Leather can be sewn on almost any machine, old or new. Sewing vinyl is not really difficult once you understand its characteristics. Leather, vinyl, and velvet require accurate stitching, since needle holes are permanent. Cotton is easier to sew and handle than the napped or pile fabrics, which slide on each other while being stitched. Satin also slides and tends to fray, but its lovely sheen makes sewing with it worth the effort. Knits stretch nicely over rounded forms. Wools are a delight to work with since they can be molded with the iron and eased while stitching. Felt does not ravel and can be cut to any shape, but will lose its shape if washed.

Many ways of coping with a tricky fabric are suggested in the text: stiffening or backing with paper; using a hoop; pinning more liberally; easing pressure on the presser foot; changing the needle size, the thread size, the stitch length. Because a certain fabric has what seem to be negative points does not mean you should not give it a try. Such points can very often be used to advantage.

As you work with fabric, you will probably find you prefer certain colors more than others, and you may decide to specialize in a particular range. However, because of changing styles and seasons, the colors you want may not always be available. To have colors when you want them, keep a stockpile on hand; save scraps

Figure 2-11. *Sunshades* by Gerhardt
Knodel. Cotton canvas and nylon marqui-
sette, screen printed and covered with
clear vinyl.

and purchase lengths you know you will eventually use. Other than that, keep searching in stores, at rummage sales, remnant counters, and through old clothes, or work with whatever colors you can find and harmonize them. You can also paint or dye fabric to the color you want.

Shopping for Fabric

The many new fibers and blends in fabric today make it difficult to tell the makeup of a piece just by its look or feel. There is no problem when buying fabric off the bolt. The information on the end of the bolt, or on its handtag, reveals fiber content, amount of expected shrinkage, and if the fabric is washable or should be drycleaned. The problem will arise when you buy an unmarked remnant.

Fabric artists are noted for constantly looking through "bolt-end/seconds" stores. They choose fabrics more for appearance and texture than for wash and wear qualities. However, there are ways to check the quality and suitability of that strange cloth you may have found on the bargain table—or, any cloth for that matter. Test its wrinkle resistance by wadding a corner in your hand, crushing it, then releasing. It will either shed its wrinkles or stay crushed. Check for excess sizing (a thickener used to give body to fabric) by rubbing two areas together. If a fine, powdery dust accumulates on the surface, too much sizing has been applied. Rubbing will also reveal if the fabric crocks (the dye comes off on your hands). Check the weave by scratching a small area in one corner.

If threads shift and separate easily, any seams stitched on the fabric may slip or develop holes around stitching lines. Unroll as much fabric as you plan to buy and check for misweaves, undyed areas, or stains. Hold it up to see how it drapes. Pull it to see how much and in which direction it stretches. Ask a salesperson for information. This may be as much as you can do in the store.

When you buy an unidentified fabric, you might try test-ironing it at various settings, starting at the lowest heat setting and progressively increasing it until the iron moves smoothly and easily over the cloth. However, because of the number of blends on the market today, it will not always be possible to determine the composition of an unmarked fabric.

Figure 2-12. Plain weaves. Burlap (*top left*), cotton canvas (*top right*), percale (*bottom*).

Figure 2-13. Patterned weaves. Double-weave faille (*top*), brocade with metallic thread (*bottom*).

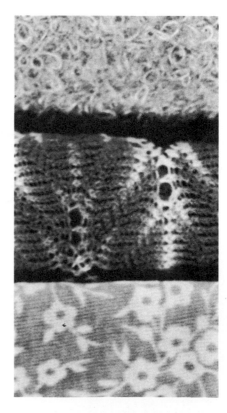

Figure 2-14. Knitted fabric. Mohair and wool (*top*), synthetic knit (*center*), cotton knit (*bottom*).

26

Fabric Chart

	Characteristics	Examples	Care
I. Natural Fibers			
Cotton	Strong, little stretch. Shrinks unless treated. Accepts dyes well.	Denim, organdy, gauze, canvas, seersucker, corduroy, velveteen.	Hand or machine wash. Iron while damp.
Linen	Stronger than cotton, little stretch. Does not lint or fray. Tends to shrink unless treated. Dyes may crock.	Damask, sailcloth, leno, gauze.	Wash with care or dry clean. Iron at high setting.
Silk	Extremely strong, highly elastic. Excellent affinity for dyes.	Chiffon, crepe, brocade, organdy, pongee, velvet, shantung.	Usually dry cleaned. Iron on wrong side at low setting.
Wool	Resilient. Shrinks. Felts naturally with heat, moisture, and pressure. Accepts dyes well.	Alpaca, mohair, gabardine, broadcloth, flannel, cashmere.	Handwash in cool water or dry clean. Block, air dry. Iron on wrong side at moderate setting.
II. Synthetic Fibers			
Acetate	Resilient, shrink and stretch resistant. Dyes unstable.	Wide range, from sheers to heavyweights. Satin, taffeta, jersey, crepe.	Wash or dry clean. Iron at low setting.
Acrylic	Unique among synthetics for aesthetic qualities. Soft, light, fluffy, strong. Resembles wool. Accepts dyes easily.	Often blended with other fibers. Knits, fleece, fake fur.	Machine wash or dry clean. Iron at low setting, if needed.
Metallic	Weak, easily stretched unless core-wrapped. Tarnishes unless plastic-coated.	Blended with other fibers for decorative purposes.	Dry clean if plastic-coated; otherwise machine wash.
Modacrylic	Strong. Excellent affinity for dyes.	Deep pile and fleece.	Dry clean deep pile; some others can be laundered. Avoid ironing.
Nylon	Exceptionally strong. Elastic, smooth. May pill.	Often blended with other fibers. Wide range from woven and knitted fabrics to washable fleece.	Washes easily, but get out all soap to avoid discoloring. Iron at low setting.
Polyester	The most outstanding synthetic fiber. High strength. May pill. Resists shrinking and stretching. Good affinity for dyes.	Many different weights and weaves. Crepe, double knit. Often blended with natural fibers.	Machine wash in warm water. Iron if needed.
Rayon	Relatively weak. Stretches or shrinks unless treated. Good affinity for dyes.	Butcher linen, matte jersey.	Dry clean or launder, depending on type. Iron on wrong side while damp.
Spandex	Strong, lightweight. Great elasticity.	Woven and knitted fabrics, medium to heavyweight. Delicate laces.	Wash in warm water. Rinse well. Drip dry.
Triacetate	Can be heat set to hold creases. Takes dye readily.	Woven and knitted fabrics, from very sheer to heavyweight.	Wash or dry clean. Iron at moderate heat.

STUFFING

Stuffing provides softness, added bulk, increased dimension, stability, and firmness to a sewn piece. Since what is inside affects how the outside looks, feels, and functions, choose stuffing according to the intended use of the project.

Several types are commonly available. Polyester fiberfill, a popular choice, is springy, washable, and wonderfully easy and satisfying to use. It comes in loose bulk or in pillow-size bags (sold by weight). Polyester batting, ½ inch to 2 inches (1.3 to 5.1 cm) thick, comes folded or rolled. These batts require close quilting to prevent the fibers from shifting when the stuffed piece is used or washed. There is less shift-

ing in bonded or glazed polyester batting; its interlocking fibers hold the stuffing in place. This material comes in various thicknesses for use in quilts and upholstery.

Loose stuffing and quilting batts also come in cotton. The cotton varies in quality from short fibers with bits of plant material left in to high-quality, long staple fibers. It is washable, stable, and long-wearing but may matt and fail to fluff up again. If used in large pieces, it should be stitched every 2 inches (5.1 cm) to prevent shifting when washed.

There are two types of foam stuffing: foam rubber, a natural latex, which is comfortable and resilient; and polyurethane foam (a synthetic), not as resilient as the rubber, but lighter in weight, less expensive, and less likely to deteriorate from use. Both types come in thin sheets and thick forms, precut to standard sizes. If you cannot find a thick foam in the shape you want, the store may cut it to your specifications. If not, cut

Figure 2-16. Stuffed figure by Dale Schumacher (19″ tall).

Figure 2-15. Wall hanging by Kathy Orzorio (24″ × 48″). Polyester fiberfill stuffing used to create a bas relief sculptural effect.

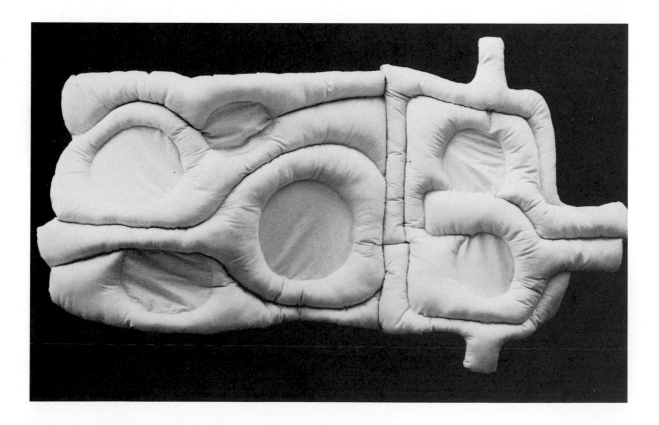

it yourself with a serrated bread knife, a hack saw, or an electric carving knife. Thin sheets can be cut with scissors or razor blade and stitched on the sewing machine (you may need to use paper, back and front, to keep the foam from sticking to the needle plate or presser foot).

Feathers make superior pillow-fillers because of their resilience, but they fly all over unless controlled while stuffing. Fiber, foam, or feathers can also be combined in one piece. For instance, polyester batting can be wrapped around a foam core (combines firmness and softness) or a foam shell can be filled with feathers (gives softness and retains shape).

Less expensive stuffings for large or experimental projects include kapok, plastic, and shredded foam. Kapok tends to fly about (make a small opening in kapok bag and take out a small amount at a time). Plastic pellets and shredded foam will cling to you (pour directly from the bag into your stitched piece). Kapok and shredded foam are not practical to wash since they take a long time to dry. In addition, you can use wadded newspaper, shredded papers, excelsior (shredded wood shavings), and plastic bags from the dry cleaner. Look around your house for old clothing, old mattress padding, and old blankets. Can you see the message coming? Throw nothing away—you can never tell when you might want to use it.

Special-effect stuffings include nylon stockings, corn (dried or popped), dried peas and beans, sand, kitty litter, shotgun pellets, pine cones, hair, stones, dried grass clippings, sticks, and dried leaves. The heavier items mentioned are often used to weigh down the bottom of an unstable piece to keep it upright. (Some of these stuffings have dreadful disadvantages: The beans might sprout and grow! But then, it depends on how you plan to use the piece—results could be spectacular.)

Cleaning Fiber Works

Good care can prolong the life of your fabric piece. Frequent dusting, or a good shaking out, will remove surface dirt before it has a chance to become embedded. To help fibers resist fingerprints or airborne dirt, spray with a fabric protector. Attend to spots and stains while they are fresh, and remove as much as you can with an absorbent cloth. For grease stains, use a dry-cleaning fluid. Follow the manufacturer's directions and be careful not to get rings. If stains remain, have the piece dry-cleaned. If the piece is preshrunk, colorfast, and can be conveniently washed, do so, first making sure that it will dry well. Some fibers may become weakened when wet, so handle with care. Stuffed pieces must be dried quickly. Air-dry, unless the piece can stand the abrasive action of the automatic dryer. Never dry or display fabric pieces in direct sunlight, unless you want them sun-bleached. If possible, remove stuffing before washing (unless stuffing is a thin layer). Machine embroidered pieces often pucker when washed; press puckers out. In general, suit the type of cleaning and treatment to the technique and materials used.

Figure 2-17. Quilt by Robin Greeson Dworkin (6' × 5'). Silk screened design on cotton velvet; polyester stuffing.

29

3. SEWING BASICS

PREPARING THE FABRIC

If you are making a piece that will be washed, preshrink the fabric first. Wash carefully, then press out any wrinkles. Check the end of the bolt (or the hangtag) before buying fabric to see if it has been preshrunk or what percent shrinkage to expect. One percent to three percent is not much, but more may make a big difference. If the fabric is wool, fragile, or dry-cleanable, roll or fold it in a damp towel, then unroll on a flat surface and allow it to dry and relax overnight. Or send it to the dry cleaner for preshrinking.

To see if the fabric is on grain, clip it on the selvage (finished side edge) and either pull out a single thread

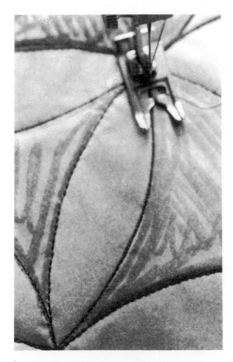

Figure 3-1. Stitching design through paper.

from selvage to selvage or quickly tear the fabric straight across. On pile or napped fabrics, unravel a thread and draw it out. Grain is the direction of the fabric threads. Those running horizontally from selvage to selvage form the crosswise grain; those running vertically form the lengthwise grain. Once a straight line has been established, fold the fabric in half, lengthwise, and line it up at the corners. If the ends are not even, the fabric is off grain. To straighten it, start at a corner and pull diagonally in the direction opposite to the off-grain slant. An alternate method is to press the fabric with a steam iron, or a dry iron and damp cloth. Bonded and permanent press fabrics have their grain heat-sealed into position during processing and cannot be straightened.

Fabric Stiffeners Soft fabric, lightweight fabric, or any fabric with little dimensional stability needs extra body to keep it from puckering. This can be provided in several ways. Paper can be pinned to the back or front of the fabric, depending on the sewing situation. Use paper that is stiff enough to be easily penetrated by the needle; typing paper and newspaper are good choices. Carefully tear paper away when sewing is completed. Spray-on starch can be ironed on the fabric, then either washed out after stitching or allowed to remain. Iron-on adhesive facing may be pressed onto the back of the fabric; trim edges away from around finished stitches if not wanted. Also, stiff fabric or layers of fabric can be pinned or basted to the back; since these will not be removable, plan them as part of your finished piece. A hoop may also be used to hold the fabric taut (see section on Hoops).

PINNING THE FABRIC

If your machine has a hinged presser foot, you can pin-baste instead of machine-baste. Insert pins on the stitch line and at right angles to it. Sew over them with the hinged presser foot. If you do not have a hinged

presser foot, put pins just short of the stitch line; or stop the machine when you reach a pin and handwheel across; or remove pins just before you reach them. *Note:* Do not try to sew over pins with either twin or triple needles since the needles will most certainly break.

When working with layered fabric, as in appliqué or quilting, make sure pins are not left where they could accidentally be sewn in place. However, if this should happen, push the sharp end of the pin out as far as it will go. If the backing is a loose weave, you should be able to work the pin out; otherwise, clip off the end with wire cutters. Never put pins on the underside of the fabric where they could come in contact with the feed. Stop instantly if you hit a pin. Remove it and change the needle; a dull needle will snag the fabric. Hitting a pin may also break the needle. Sometimes the needle will bend a pin and push it down the needle hole where it might jam the machine.

If you have placed a lot of pins in a fairly large piece, roll it to leave exposed only the part you will be stitching at the moment. This keeps the pins safely in place and the bulk of the fabric out of the way. Also consider using safety pins to hold the rolled material; they are less prickly and hold the material more securely than straight pins.

THREADING THE MACHINE

All sewing machines have the same main parts essential to forming a simple stitch, and each part must be threaded in the proper order. If you understand the role that each plays, you will always remember how to thread your machine.

The *top thread* is placed on the spool pin and is drawn through a thread guide or guides (the number varies with each machine); the purpose of the guides, here and elsewhere, is to control an even, untangled flow of thread. The thread then goes to the tension discs and is slipped between them. Pressure on these discs is regulated by the top thread tension control. This control is probably the most important one on the machine, since stitch appearance depends on the amount of pressure the discs exert on the thread. From the discs, the thread goes through the eyelet in the take-up lever and then down to the needle. The lever, moving up and down on each stitch, regulates the flow of thread to the needle.

The *bottom thread* is wound on the bobbin in a manner that varies with the type of bobbin and the type of sewing machine. The wound bobbin rests freely in the bobbin case and revolves within it, while the case remains in place in a hollow ring called a shuttle. On most bobbin cases, there is a small adjustable screw for regulating bobbin tension.

How a stitch is actually formed, in case you have always wondered, is shown in Figure 3-2.

THREADING THE NEEDLE

For as long as needles have been in existence, stitchers have been poking thread hopefully at that tiny eye; some have even tried inventing easier ways to thread it. One popular aid is a diamond-shaped wire with a flat handle. Other aids are incorporated into some sewing machines, and include needle threading from the front, a built-in light aimed at the needle, and a presser foot with a white shank to make the eye more

visible. If you place your thumbnail next to the eye at an angle, it will show the eye clearly and act as a thread guide. An easy way to guide a heavy thread through the needle is to cut a 4 to 6 inch (10.2 to 15.2 cm) length of regular (50) thread, double it, and insert both ends in the eye. Put the heavy thread in the resulting loop and pull the ends (and the heavy thread) through. This simulates the wire needle threader.

Be sure auxiliary light around the machine is bright and non-glaring. Also keep a small magnifying glass, or a large illuminated one, next to the machine for additional help if needed. Or you could wear a pair of magnifying eyeglasses as some hand embroiderers or stamp collectors do.

Insert the needle as specified in your manual. It must be all the way up into its slot on the needle bar. When threading the needle, turn the handwheel toward you and bring the take-up lever to its highest point. This in turn will raise the needle to its highest position, the best position for threading. With a sharp scissors (of course, your scissors are sharp), clip the thread at an angle. The thread cutter on the machine is wonderfully convenient for cutting thread during stitching but does not cut a sharp enough end for needle threading. If the thread end is frayed or raveled, make a firmer point by dampening thumb and forefinger and rolling the thread between them in the direction of its twist. Push the end through the eye and continue to

hold the thread as you slide your fingers past the needle. This should help guide it all the way through. Catch it on the far side and pull through at least 6 or 7 inches (15.2 or 17.8 cm).

To thread twin needles, place thread on both spool pins or, if your machine has just one spool pin, put one spool in a container placed on the machine bed and pass the thread around the spool pin to anchor it. Feed the threads through the machine, either separately or at the same time, whichever works for you. Some machines have guides for two threads on the needle shaft, but if yours does not, thread both through the same guide. A single bobbin thread twines around both top threads. Triple needles are threaded in the same manner.

Figure 3-2. How a stitch is formed.

(1) Needle brings top thread through fabric and into bobbin case area.

(2) As needle begins its upstroke, it leaves a loop of thread behind for shuttle hook to catch.

(3) Shuttle hook carries loop around and under bobbin case.

(4) As needle rises higher, the take-up lever exerts its pull on top thread; loop slips off hook and bobbin case, goes around bobbin thread.

(5) Take-up lever pulls both threads up into a lockstitch. Feed moves forward to advance fabric; needle begins downstroke for next stitch.

HOW A STITCH IS FORMED

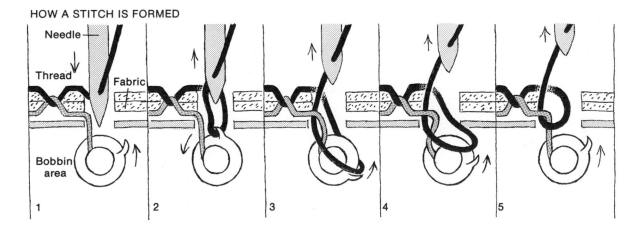

STARTING TO SEW

To bring up the bobbin thread, hold the needle thread loosely in your left hand and turn the handwheel slowly toward you in one complete turn. In that turn, the top thread will catch the bobbin thread and bring it up in a loop. Pull gently on the top thread and bring the bobbin thread all the way through. Draw up at least 3 inches (7.6 cm) and pass both threads under the presser foot. The machine is now ready for sewing.

Place the fabric under the raised presser foot and adjust it so that stitching will begin ¼ to ½ inches (.6 to 1.3 cm) from the top edge. Lower the presser foot lever. Whether or not a presser foot is used, *always* lower the presser foot lever; threads under no tension will snarl in the bobbin case. Begin sewing with the take-up lever at its highest position or with a long thread pulled from the needle, so the needle will not become unthreaded at the first stitch. As an extra precaution, hold thread ends together when starting the first stitch.

Stitch at an even speed, without slowing up or rushing ahead. Watch the stitch as it is formed. Let the fabric feed freely and see that it is aligned with the machine guidelines.

Figure 3-3. Fingers positioned in front and to the side of presser foot.

Reduce speed as you near the end of the stitch line so that you do not go beyond it.

When starting to sew a seam that will not be intersected by another seam, lock the threads by sewing in reverse (backstitch) for two or three stitches or to the top edge of the fabric. At the end of the seam, backstitch to fasten.

GUIDING THE FABRIC

As you sew, hold the fabric lightly with the fingertips of both hands—one hand in front of the presser foot, the other to its left. Usually this is sufficient to maintain smooth, even stitching in most fabrics. Some fabrics, such as sheers, crepes, and knits, may need to be held both in front and in back of the presser foot. When sewing in the body of the fabric, hold it lightly on both sides of the presser foot.

Guidelines on the throat plate are spaced at intervals of ⅛ inch (.3 cm). It will help you stitch a straight seam if you line up the fabric edge with one of the guidelines and keep the edge along the line as you stitch. When stitching a narrow seam, you can align the fabric with the edge of the presser foot. For a seam wider than machine guidelines allow, put a piece of masking tape on the machine bed at the distance you need, and align the fabric with the edge of the tape.

Detachable guides, such as seam guides and quilting bars, are also available; they aid in stitching a uniform distance from the edge, from another line, or as close to an edge as possible. The seam guide screws into either of two threaded holes in the machine bed, and can be adjusted to various seam widths. There are several types, including one that is held in place with a magnet. The quilting bar is attached to the presser foot and extends out from it. By adjusting the guide to fall along a previously stitched line, you can make a parallel row of stitches.

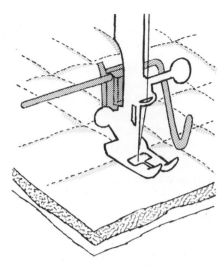

Figure 3-4. Adjustable quilting bar. Placed either to right or left of needle, keeps stitching rows parallel.

PRESSER FOOT PRESSURE, STITCH LENGTH, AND STITCH TENSION

Presser foot pressure, stitch length, and stitch tension are three variables that must be adjusted to the specific fabric used. Before starting any sewing project, make it a habit to test the stitches, using the same fabric and number of layers, as well as the correct needle and thread.

Adjusting Pressure. The pressure exerted on the fabric by the presser foot is regulated by the pressure control. The amount of pressure required will vary according to fabric type and weight. As a rule, increase pressure when sewing lightweight fabrics and decrease it when sewing heavyweight fabrics or multiple layers. If thick, soft, or very stretchy fabrics do not feed smoothly, pressure is too light. If fabric ripples, pressure is too heavy. Pressure is also adjusted for certain stitching techniques.

Adjusting Stitch Length. The distance that the fabric moves on each stitch is regulated by the stitch length control. Generally, longer stitches are used for thick fabrics or multiple layers; shorter stitches for lighter weight fabrics.

Adjusting Tension: Balanced Stitches. The strongest machine-sewn stitch is a balanced one. Top and bottom threads are drawn equally into the fabric and lock in the center of the work. You achieve a balanced stitch by adjusting the tension controls. These controls regulate the amount of pressure exerted on the top and bottom threads. Pressure on the needle thread is regulated by the top tension control: the higher the number, the tighter the tension. Most tension adjustments are made from this control. When adjusting top tension, do so with the presser foot down; tension discs are open when the foot is up.

If the top thread lies straight on the face of the fabric with the bottom

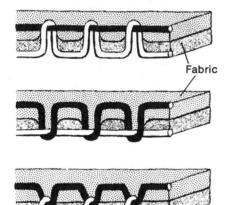

Figure 3-5. Top thread too tight (*top*). Top thread too loose (*center*). Balanced stitches (*bottom*).

thread looping over it, tension is too tight; loosen top tension slightly. If the bottom thread lies straight on the underside of the fabric with the top thread looping over it, tension is too loose; tighten top tension slightly. If the fabric puckers, both top and bottom tensions are too tight; loosen top tension slightly. If the fabric still puckers, try adjusting the stitch length. If the stitch is satisfactory, but the fabric still puckers, you may have to loosen the bobbin tension.

The tension control for the bobbin thread, if the machine has one, is a

small screw located on the tension slot of the bobbin case. This control requires adjustment much less frequently than does the top thread control. When adjusting, do so after the bobbin case has been threaded; use the small screwdriver that came with your machine for this purpose. A minute adjustment is all that is necessary; even a very slight turn will make a noticeable difference in the stitch.

To increase tension, turn the screw clockwise. To decrease tension, turn the screw counterclockwise. Be careful when decreasing tension that the screw does not fall out and get lost. On some sewing machines, bobbin tension is preset at the factory and manufacturers do not encourage adjustments.

TRIMMING FOR TURNING

Careful attention to inside seams can make a great difference in the appearance of a stuffed piece. A bulky seam, or one that pulls, can distort the shape by lumping or wrinkling.

Curves. For an outward (convex) curve, trim one seam allowance shorter than the other to avoid a double thickness at the seamline. This step is necessary if the piece will be pressed and might show the seam as a ridge on the outside, or if the extra fabric will appear as bumps in the stuffing. Make

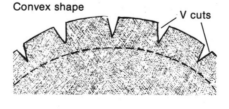

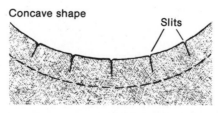

Figure 3-6. Notched outward curve (*top*). Slashed inward curve (*bottom*).

little V-shaped cuts (notches) almost to the seamline so the seam will lie flat. For an inward (concave) curve, trim one or both seams if necessary, then make slashes almost to the seamline; space the intervals according to the degree of curve and the firmness of the fabric. This allows the edges to spread out and fit the curve.

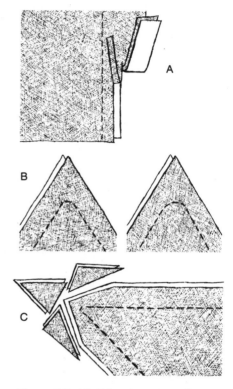

Figure 3-7. (*A*) Trimming seam allowances to various widths to reduce bulk. (*B*) Diagonal stitches make corners easier to turn. (*C*) Snipping off point and tapering sides reduces bulk.

Corners. Taking a diagonal stitch or two across the point of a corner makes turning easier and provides more space for inside seams (see Figure 3-7, B). Trim an outward corner by cutting diagonally across the point very close to the stitching. If the turned corner is still bulky or if stitches are pulling too tightly, taper each side of the diagonal cut. For inward corners, make careful slashes just up to the stitches. Much strain occurs at these corners, so you may wish to reinforce them with additional stitches. The second row must be stitched exactly over the first row.

TRANSFERRING DESIGNS

Designs can be transferred to fabric in a number of ways; the ones most generally used are given here.

Materials. Any of the following may be used for transferring: tracing paper of various sizes, typing paper, dressmakers' carbon paper, brown wrapping paper, soft lead pencil, chalk pencil, tailors' chalk.

Lead pencil lines are difficult to erase, but they wash out. Draw them on the fabric face only if they will be covered by the stitches; otherwise, draw on the back (except on sheers, since lines will show through). A chalk pencil, sharpened to a fine point, makes a precise line on almost any fabric; marks wash out easily and brush out fairly well. The pencil comes in several colors and has a brush eraser. Tailors' chalk comes in squares of several colors; marks rub off easily, which can either be useful or a problem.

A sliver from a bar of soap is good for dark fabrics; marks do not rub off easily, but can be steam-ironed out. Ink markers come in permanent and temporary inks. The permanent ink may exude a ring or stain; the temporary ink may bleed into the design. Even so, there may be times when you will want to use these markers.

Design. First make a sketch of the design to the correct proportions. Draw just the main lines; it is not necessary to include every detail. If the sketch is full size, transfer it to the fabric; otherwise make a full-size drawing, or draw freehand for a spontaneous effect. When design shapes are simple and/or repetitive, you can cut them out of paper or cardboard and draw their outlines on the fabric. If you need help in making your design full size, or if you are adapting a design that has to be enlarged or reduced in size, use the following method.

Enlarging or Reducing Design. To enlarge a design (or to make a full-size drawing), place the design on a larger piece of paper, line up the edges, and draw a diagonal line (Figure 3-9). At the point on the diagonal that represents the desired size of the design, draw vertical and horizontal lines accordingly. To reduce a design, place a small piece of paper or tracing paper over the design, draw a diagonal line, and stop at the point you wish established as the height. Draw vertical and horizontal lines accordingly.

Mark the design off into squares (or grids), dividing it first into halves, then into quarters, then to scale. For example, you could choose a scale of 1 inch = 2 inches (2 cm=5 cm) or 1 inch = ½ inch (2 cm=1 cm) which means that every inch of the sketch

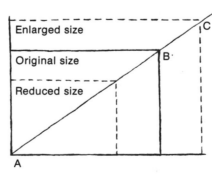

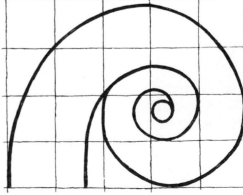

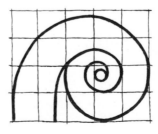

Figure 3-9. Enlarging or reducing a design. *To enlarge,* draw diagonal from *A* to *B,* then to desired size (*C*); draw height and width lines. *To reduce,* place smaller piece of paper on sketch and draw diagonal from *A* to desired size. Draw same number of squares on larger (to enlarge) or smaller (to reduce) paper and copy design, square by square.

Figure 3-8. Chalk pencil and serrated tracing wheel.

would be equal to every 2 inches or every ½ inch in the full-size drawing. Draw the same number of grids on the larger (or smaller) piece of paper, but in proportionately larger (or smaller) grids. Then copy the design, square by square.

Also, if you have the proper equipment, you can take a slide of your design and project it to a larger or smaller size by means of a slide projector. You can then draw the design on paper or directly onto the fabric. This method works best for large projects such as quilts or wall hangings. Photostating or photocopying are other methods that can be used for either your design or for a design that you are duplicating from another source. Call local print shops for prices.

Transferring Methods

The full-size design can be transferred by any of the following methods:

1. Turn the design face down and, with a soft lead pencil, tailors' chalk, or chalk pencil, go over the lines showing through to the back; bear down heavily. Turn design face up, pin it to the fabric, and trace over the lines again. Check to see if the lines have transferred before removing the design. This method works best on smooth fabrics.

2. For a direct transfer, use dressmakers' carbon paper. Place it, carbon side down, between the fabric and the design. Pin or tape in place and go over the lines with a tracing wheel or blunt pencil. Check to see if lines have transferred before removing the design.

3. If the design is not too large and the fabric is sheer or lightweight, you can use the light method. Place the design, face up, on a light box or tape it to a window. Tape the fabric over the design. With the light coming through from the back, trace lines onto the fabric with pencil or chalk.

4. If you plan to use a design several times, you can make a perforated pattern. Draw the design on typing paper or heavy tracing paper and sew over the lines with an unthreaded machine. Pin the design to the fabric. With a pounce bag (made of porous material and containing chalk dust) or with loose chalk dust and a rolled pad of felt, rub the dust into the holes until dotted chalk lines appear on the fabric.

5. The design can also be outlined with stitches. Draw the design on thin tracing paper, pin it to the fabric face and machine baste around the outlines. Or, pin it to the back, with the design facing the fabric, and baste from that side. Carefully remove the paper (dampen for easier removal and use tweezers) so as not to pull the stitches. Or keep the paper in place throughout the stitching, then remove it; in this way, it will also serve to stabilize the fabric.

6. If you want to work from the back of the fabric, but do not want a mirror image to appear on the front, make a reverse drawing—trace the design on tracing paper, turn the paper over and retrace the lines on the wrong side. Transfer or pin this tracing to the back of the fabric.

7. If you want a permanent backing on the fabric, make a reverse drawing and trace it onto organdy, batiste, or iron-on interfacing. Pin the drawing to the back of the fabric, design face up, and stitch in place. Or, machine baste the lines, turn the fabric over, and stitch on the face side. Remove basting.

8. If the fabric is coarsely woven, you can lay netting over the design and trace the lines with an ink marker. Pin netting to the fabric and retrace lines with the marker or with chalk. The ink, or chalk, will pass through the holes of the netting and onto the fabric. Or, cut the design shapes out of paper, pin them to the fabric, and stitch around the outlines.

Figure 3-10. Design sketched with ink marker.

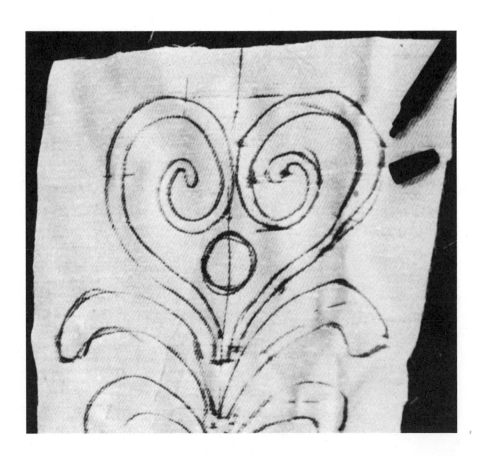

4. EMBROIDERY

If you can straight-stitch, you can machine-embroider. If your machine can do the zigzag stitch as well, then the possibilities for design are greater still. The capability of these two basic stitches to create all sorts of linear designs is responsible in part for the widespread appeal of machine embroidery. The added attraction is free-motion stitching, accomplished by disengaging the feed so that the fabric is released and moves freely under the needle. Your hands guide the cloth as the machine "draws" patterns in continuous lines. With this type of stitching, you can use straight, zigzag, or automatic stitches.

For those attempting the techniques for the first time, practice is essential in order to learn how to control the machine and to become familiar with some of the many stitch variations that can be produced. Once you know the basics, you can experiment freely. Before starting a project, make a sampler to find the best combination of thread, needle, fabric, thread tension, and presser foot pressure.

STRAIGHT STITCH

Any sewing machine, from an old treadle to an inexpensive portable to a top-of-the-line model, can straight-stitch. The most common use of this stitch is to sew a seam or join together two or more layers of fabric. But it can also outline a shape on fabric or describe lines that resemble pencil drawings. Using no more than straight or curved lines, you can make handsome geometric patterns (including plaids) and decorative designs, as well as embroidery. By trying different weight threads, combining colors, and altering thread

tension, you can create a variety of interpretations. To start you on your way, here is the basic information you need to know.

Stitching Corners. To turn a square corner, as in a rectangular shape, stitch down one side to the point of turning. Stop the machine, leave the needle in the fabric, and raise the presser foot. Pivot the fabric on the needle and make a right-angle turn. Lower the presser foot and continue stitching. To turn a sharp corner, as in a triangular shape, pivot the fabric until it heads in the direction of the new stitch line. In both cases, turn the fabric gently so that it does not bunch up under the needle. Also, so that you do not stitch beyond it, slow down before reaching the turn, or use the handwheel to take the last stitch or two.

Stitching Curves. Guide the fabric gently along the drawn curved line. For better control, run the machine at a slower speed than for straight lines. If you have a seam guide, place it at the angle of the curve.

Stitching Circles. Some sewing machines have special needle plates for stitching perfect circles, but you can also make your own circle guide with a thumbtack and masking tape (Figure 4-2). First decide on the circle size, then find the radius by measuring the distance from the center of the circle to the outside edge. Measure the same distance from the left side of the needle and tape the thumbtack there, pointed end up. Position the fabric on the tack so that the point penetrates the center of the desired circle. Put a cork or an eraser on the point to hold the fabric in place. Insert the needle

Figure 4-1. Straight stitch sampler.

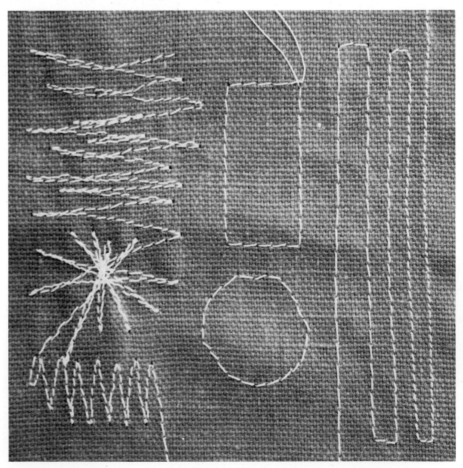

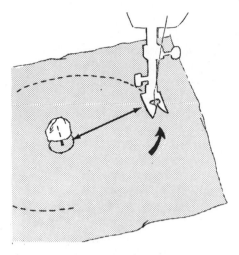

Figure 4-2. Homemade circle guide. An upended thumbtack secured with masking tape; cork or eraser holds fabric in place on tack.

on the stitch line and begin stitching. Hold the fabric taut as you stitch, but not tightly, and guide it slowly and carefully. It is usually not necessary to back the fabric when straight-stitching, but if it should bunch up while being turned, back it with paper, then gently remove the paper when the circle is completed.

Practice Stitching Lines and Shapes

An excellent way to practice stitching straight lines, curves, and corners is with a sheet of paper and an unthreaded machine. Since needle penetrations are so obvious, you can easily see when a stitch strays from a line.

Try this .... Draw a series of parallel lines on typing or lined paper. Lower the needle and presser foot and follow along the first line. At the end of the line, move to another line. Continue in this fashion, guiding the paper carefully and raising needle and presser foot whenever you change position. Go slowly at first to make sure that all the needle holes march neatly on the line, then stitch with a little more speed.

Next, draw a rectangle and practice turning corners. You can also try a series of rectangles enclosing other rectangles of increasing or decreasing sizes. To make one kind of geometric pattern, draw a series of parallel lines, spaced either evenly or unevenly. Follow along the first line. At the bottom of the line, make a right-angle turn and stitch to meet the next line. Turn again and stitch in the new direction. Continue in this fashion. Then practice curves and circles, moving the paper so that the needle follows along the drawn lines. Stitch a spiral, or make ever-increasing circles. See if you can control the distance between each circle.

Experimenting with Straight Stitch

Draw lines and shapes as before, but this time on fabric. Use a contrasting color thread in the machine so the stitches can be clearly seen.

Begin stitching. Remember to slow down when nearing a corner or a sharp dip in a curve. Guide the fabric and keep it smooth. When you think you have done a good job, start experimenting.

Try this .... Combine the lines and shapes; make radiating lines, oblique lines and a series of overlapping curves. Then try moving the fabric in various directions as you stitch, doing so slowly, without pulling or tugging. Move from side to side, in wavy lines, in circles, in spirals. Stitch both forward and backward. Use different stitch lengths. You will soon discover how versatile this stitch is and how it can be controlled to create a great variety of patterns.

The straight stitch sampler (Figure 4-1) can serve as guide for your beginning experiments.

1. Parallel Lines. Set stitch length control to the finest setting on your machine and stitch the first row (extreme right). At the end of the row make a right-angle turn. Repeat the turn for the next corner. Increase stitch length for subsequent rows. The last row made will be the longest stitch setting on your machine.

2. Rectangle and Circle. Make the first and last stitches in the same stitch hole or as close together as possible. At completion, pull thread ends through to the back and tie in a knot to secure the stitching.

3. Random Stitching. Stitch forward and in reverse (use reverse button or lever) and move the fabric to the left or right when reversing.

When you have completed several samplers of straight stitch patterns, see how they look when worked with a variety of thread colors. You can then go on to experiment with decorative threads and yarns. Notice how the use of different weights and types of threads alters stitch appearance.

Figure 4-3. Detail on tie by Ellen Toby Holmes. Straight stitch embroidery, forward and in reverse.

DECORATIVE THREADS

Not all threads are wound on spools; some of them, including yarns and some embroidery threads, come on tubes or cones, or in balls or skeins. If the dispenser fits on the spool pin, the thread can be fed through the machine in the usual manner. However, most dispensers are not so accommodating.

When using a cone, try placing it over a large spool of thread on the spool pin so that it rides on the spool and unwinds easily. If this cannot be done, set the cone in front of the machine, pass the thread around the spool pin to anchor it, and thread it through the thread guides and tension discs in the usual manner. A cone has a wide base and can sit quite steadily; but if your machine rattles it about, set the cone in a basket or other container placed next to the machine (on a chair or on the floor). A tube or ball of thread can be similarly placed and then fed through the machine. An alternate method for feeding thread through the machine from a cone or large spool is to use a thread stand (Figure 4-5). The dispenser is set on a spool pin at the base of the stand, the thread is passed through a guide at the top, and is then threaded through the machine.

You could also wind thread or yarn on a bobbin and place that on the spool pin. To do this, put a bobbin on the bobbin winder (remember to disengage the clutch knob), hold the dispenser with one hand and, with the other hand, guide the feeding onto the bobbin. If the dispenser is large or unwieldy, fit a knitting needle, dowel, or pencil through its center and unwind in this manner. Transfer the threaded bobbin to the spool pin and thread through as usual.

Thick threads, embroidery floss, elastic thread, string, cord, yarn, novelty wools, and other decorative threads can all be tried. Those too heavy to pass through the eye of the needle can be wound on a bobbin and used as the bottom thread. (If you want the bottom thread to appear on the face of the fabric, work with the underside of the fabric up.) However, not all threads can be machine-wound on a bobbin. Some, such as elastic cord, embroidery floss, and thick yarns, have to be hand-wound. Wind these carefully, without twisting or bunching up, and not too tightly. If threads are thick, do not fill the bobbin completely or it will be too fat to fit into the bobbin case.

Some threads may be too thick to pass through the bobbin tension spring at its normal setting, so al-

Figure 4-4. (*Above*) *The Voices of Spring* by Verina Warren (12″ × 9″). Illustrates rich use of decorative threads, including gold thread. (*Right*) Detail of lower portion.

ternative methods have to be found. One is to loosen the screw that controls bobbin tension (some machines have a "finger" which exerts minimal pressure on the bobbin thread and allows the use of thick threads and yarns). Another way is to bypass bobbin tension altogether. Consult your manual for information; if there is none, you will have to experiment. Some machines will not allow the tension spring to be bypassed, others have a hole in the bobbin case for the thread to pass through. On still others, you may be able to bypass tension like a charm one day and, on the next, not be able to do it at all. If a thread or yarn is too large to dispense easily from the bobbin, couch it onto the fabric (see Couching).

Experimenting with Decorative Threads and Altered Tension

You have already learned how to adjust top and bottom thread tension to achieve a balanced stitch. Thread tension can also be purposely altered to "unbalance" a stitch. These unbalanced or altered tension stitches can be used to create a type of couching in which one machine-sewn thread couches the other. Try the sampler suggestions that follow.

Needle Thread Sampler

Thread the machine, top and bottom, with regular size (50) thread in contrasting colors. Aim first for a balanced stitch. Then tighten the top tension control. Continue tightening it until the bobbin thread comes to the surface. The looser bobbin thread will loop around the tighter top thread, "couching" it. Stitch in various directions to see what can be achieved. This type of seam may not be as strong as one made with balanced stitches, but it can be more decorative.

Next, experiment with other threads. Try heavy duty thread, buttonhole twist, crochet cord, embroidery thread, or whatever will work in the top of your machine

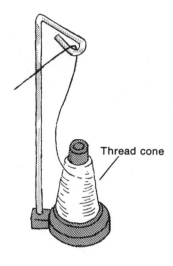

Thread cone

Figure 4-5. Thread stand. An alternate way to support a large spool or cone of thread.

(leave the regular thread on the bobbin). Use a needle with an eye large enough to accommodate the thread. Stitch to see if the needle/thread/fabric combination will work. If necessary, change the fabric, change the thread, change the needle, or back the fabric with paper to stiffen it. Tighten the top tension to achieve the proper adjustment (neither too tight nor too loose), then start stitching. Note how altering the tension changes the design quality and texture of the stitches.

Bobbin Thread Sampler

For this technique, just work in reverse. The heavy thread goes in the bobbin, the regular thread in the needle, and the top tension is loosened. The advantage to this technique is that a greater assortment of threads, yarns, and string can be used. This includes threads that might shred when passed through the needle (such as metallic thread and some yarns), or that are too thick for the needle, or not strong enough to withstand the tightened tension. The disadvantage is that you will not be able to see the stitches as they are being formed and will have to look on the underside of the fabric to know what is happening.

When the machine is threaded, loosen the top tension until the looser top thread is couching the tighter bobbin thread. While stitching, note the difference in stitch appearance between this technique and the previous one. If some threads cannot pass through the bobbin tension spring, bypass the spring if you can, or loosen the bobbin tension screw. If you plan to do a lot of work with heavy threads in the bobbin, consider buying an extra bobbin case to use just for experimenting.

For an exaggerated altered stitch, turn the top tension to 0. Long, looped stitches that only loosely hold the bobbin thread will appear on the underside of the fabric. Secure these loops by applying an adhesive such as fabric glue, iron-on interfacing, or liquid rubber (the type used for rugs) to the top side. Turn the fabric to the underside and pull out the loose bobbin thread. With this technique, you can make a row of closely spaced loops or fringe.

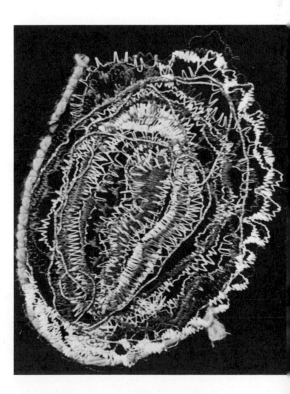

Figure 4-6. *Experimental Doodle* by Joann T. Szymanski (6" × 24"). Decorative threads, yarns, and altered tension.

ZIGZAG STITCH

Zigzag stitches have a side-to-side width (called bight) as well as a stitch length. This side-to-side distance that the needle travels on each stitch is regulated by the stitch width control. The higher the number, the wider the stitch (the 0 setting results in a straight stitch). Stitch length can be varied from a long zigzag of about 6 stitches per inch to one so closely spaced it is called satin stitch. Tension is regulated in the same manner as for straight stitching, but the zigzag stitch requires a looser top tension. (Some machines also have a needle position control that sets the needle in three positions: left of center, center, right of center.)

Zigzag Stitch Sampler

As can be seen in the sampler in Figure 4-7, stitch length and width can be adjusted to produce a variety of designs. The settings provided for the stitch rows are intended as guides for your own experiments. Different models of sewing machines vary in their settings, some being capable of producing a wider bight or fewer stitches per inch than others. On some machines, stitch length is calibrated in millimeters. The higher the number, the longer the stitch.

Row 1. Stitch length: 12. Stitch width: 5 (or widest setting).

Rows 2 - 6. Stitch length: from 20 (or highest setting) to 6. Stitch width: increase by one for each row, starting with width 1 for Row 2 and ending with width 5 for Row 6. Move stitch length control at regular intervals to achieve graduated increases in length.

Row 7. Stitch length: vary from 15 to 20. Stitch width: 5. Move stitch length control back and forth.

Row 8. Stitch length: fine (the area beyond the shortest setting). Stitch width: 4. This stitch length produces a satin stitch; stitch width can vary. To do this exercise using more widely spaced stitches, adjust stitch length control.

Turning open corners, square corners and sharp curves. To make an open corner, stop with the needle inserted on the side where the turn will be made: to turn left, stop on the left side; to turn right, stop on the right side. Raise the presser foot, pivot fabric on the needle, lower foot, and continue stitching. To make a square corner, stop with needle inserted on the side *opposite* to where the turn will be made: to turn left, stop on the right side; to turn right, stop on the left side. Raise presser foot, pivot fabric on the needle, lower foot and stitch *over* the stitches in the corner. For a curve, make stitches close enough together so that they do not "open up" at the turns.

Row 9. Stitch length: fine. Stitch width: 1 to 5. Guide fabric with your left hand and move stitch width control with your right (or as your machine requires). Varying the width in this manner creates a stitch that flows like a brush stroke.

Row 10. Stitch length: varied. Stitch width: varied. Stitching this row is a slower process than stitching Row 9 because you have to manipulate both stitch length and stitch width controls, as well as guide the fabric. Unless you have three hands, you will have to stop stitching to make one adjustment or another.

Row 11. Stitch length: 12. Stitch width: 5. The same setting as Row 1,

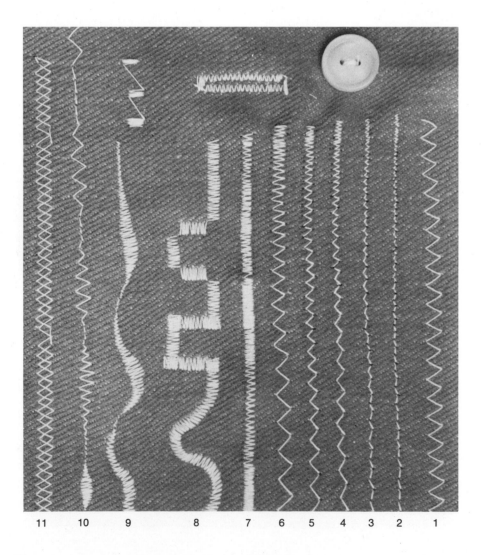

11   10   9   8   7   6   5   4   3   2   1

Figure 4-7. Zigzag stitch sampler.

but here a second row is stitched over the first. Imagine how many patterns can be created by changing stitch width and length and/or thread color and size.

Bar Tacks. Stitch length: fine. Stitch width: any width (5 was used here). Three bar tacks are shown (above Row 9) with the thread between them unclipped. On some designs, the thread can be carried from one motif to the next to avoid tying thread ends. Bar tacks are made by taking 4 or 5 stitches in the same place and can be used to sew on buttons to secure the ends of button holes, or to quilt layers together.

Button. Stitch length: fine. Stitch width: depends on space between holes. Use a button foot or zigzag foot. Lower feed (if your machine allows it); this is an advantage, but not absolutely necessary. Align holes with slot of presser foot and lower foot (with zigzag foot, hold button in place with fingers to begin). Adjust stitch width so that the needle enters the first hole; turn the handwheel so that the needle enters second hole. Stitch a number of times. Clip threads, draw to reverse side, and tie.

Buttonhole. Stitch length: fine. Stitch width: 2 and 5. Make a bar tack at width 5, change to 2 and stitch one side. Stop with the needle on the outside edge, turn fabric and repeat the whole process for other side. Open the buttonhole with a seam ripper or razor blade, or double it and clip with scissors. Buttonholes can be used as decorative openings for threads or ribbons.

Circles. (not shown). For technique, see Stitching Circles. If the stitches pucker the fabric, back with paper or use a hoop to hold the fabric taut. (See Hoops)

Altered tension stitches can also be made with the zigzag stitch. The procedure is the same as with the straight stitch, except that stitch width can be adjusted. (Also see Free Motion Altered Stitches.)

Key to Sampler		
Row	*Stitch Per Inch*	*Stitch Width*
1	12	5
2	20 to 6	1
3	20 to 6	2
4	20 to 6	3
5	20 to 6	4
6	20 to 6	5
7	15 to 20	5
8	fine (20+)	4
9	fine (20+)	1 to 5
10	20 to 6	1 to 5
11	12	5
bar tacks	fine (20+)	5
button	fine (20+)	3 to 5 (depending on button)
buttonhole	fine (20+)	2 and 5

Combining Straight and Zigzag Stitches

Doodling on fabric is one way to achieve spontaneity while stitching. Combining straight and zigzag stitches in a doodle sampler may result in a delightful design, or it may just please you to know that you can accomplish certain effects.

Try this.... For each doodle sampler, use a stiff or backed fabric, at least 12 inches (30.5 cm) square. Try various fabrics. Use a zigzag or special purpose foot.

Work the straight stitch at various lengths and the zigzag at various lengths and widths. Try moving the fabric about while varying the settings. Adjust top tension control for different results. When you find a pattern you like, see how it looks with other types and colors of thread. Also note how stitch appearance changes with varying length, width, and tension settings so that you can make use of this knowledge at another time. Figure 4-6 shows an experimental doodle made with straight, zigzag, pattern, and altered stitches.

Figure 4-8. Zigzag altered tension stitches on reverse side of fabric. Heavy thread in bobbin, top tension loosened.

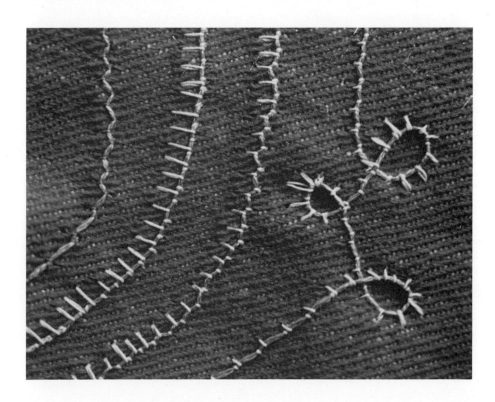

HOOPS

For certain embroidery techniques, the fabric is held taut in an embroidery hoop. Plastic and wooden hoops made especially for machine work are skinnier than those used for hand embroidery. The plastic ones can be slipped more easily under the raised needle, but the wooden ones come in larger sizes. When using a hoop (this includes hand-embroidery hoops), position fabric *over* the larger ring and snap

Figure 4-9. Position fabric over larger hoop ring, secure with smaller ring. Place under the needle so that fabric lays flat against machine bed. Note that the inner ring is wrapped with fabric tape to keep fabric from slipping.

in the smaller ring. It helps to wrap the smaller ring with fabric tape to keep fabric from slipping. Pull the fabric taut and keep it tightly stretched throughout the stitching. Be sure the fabric grain runs straight all the way across.

Bring the needle to its highest position and raise the presser foot. Slip the hoop under the needle, *fabric side down*. If the presser foot lever on your machine does not raise the foot high enough to clear the hoop, remove the foot, insert the hoop and replace the foot. If the hoop is deep (as is the case with hand-embroidery hoops), tip it on its side in order to slide it under the needle. If it is too deep for this, you may have to remove the foot, and the needle as well. It also helps to lower the feed until the hoop is positioned.

Draw the bobbin thread up through the fabric by holding the top thread in your left hand and turning

the handwheel with your right. Hold both ends and take a stitch at the spot where you wish stitching to begin. Lock the ends by sewing a few stitches in place or by backstitching. After you have taken the first few stitches, cut the excess ends, so that you will not stitch over them.

During the stitching, hold the hoop with your fingertips, thumbs at the front (see Figure 4-10). Guide the hoop by moving it with both hands. Try not to move too quickly. Also be sure that the hoop does not catch on the edge of the machine bed or the needle plate.

If the entire design is not enclosed in the hoop and you have to move the fabric to a new section, remove the hoop from under the needle, release the fabric, and reposition it. If you had to take off the presser foot (and possibly the needle) to remove the hoop, reposition the fabric while the hoop remains under the needle.

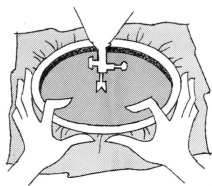

Figure 4-10. Hold hoop with fingertips, thumbs at the front, and move it with both hands.

SATIN STITCH

Satin stitching is a series of closely spaced zigzag stitches that form a smooth, satin-like surface. The stitches provide colorful outlines as well as bold patterns with raised surfaces. They are also used to decoratively finish a raw edge.

You will have to experiment to find just the right stitch length setting and top thread tension. What you are after are closely spaced, straight-edged satin stitches with no visible gaps, stitch pile-up, or fabric pucker. Stretch a piece of scrap fabric in a hoop, or back it with paper, or use a fabric stiffener. For best results when sewing over the raised stitches, use a special-purpose presser foot, if you have one; if not, use the zigzag foot and ease presser foot pressure slightly.

Decide on a stitch width and set the control. Set the stitch length to almost 0, or as near to 0 as is possible without stopping the action of the feed. Stitch at a slow speed and adjust the length gradually as you sew. Stop occasionally to see results: then start up again until stitches are the ideal distance apart. When satin stitches are closely spaced, they form a solid line.

Satin stitch usually requires a looser top tension than other zigzag stitches. If the fabric puckers, or if the bobbin thread can be seen on the fabric surface, decrease tension. Also the wider the stitch, the looser the tension must be. This results in a slightly unbalanced stitch. Because

of this, the stitch is best done from the face side of the fabric (if done on the reverse, the face side will show the worst results of unbalanced stitching).

The best threads for satin stitch are cotton embroidery thread for flexibility and/or rayon embroidery thread for luster. Heavy threads will work up faster. When changing from one type thread to another, adjust stitch width and length accordingly. Darning thread is usually used in the bobbin, but other threads can be tried as well. Since the thread will not be visible, you can choose an inexpensive grade if you wish.

Many lovely patterns will develop if you move the stitch width control as you stitch. Lines can be stitched in varied widths to resemble gracefully executed brush strokes (see Figure 4-7 Row 9). Monograms or names are particularly effective when satin-stitched in varied widths.

Figure 4-11. *Butterfly* by Yvanne Ham (4" × 4"). Satin stitch embroidery. Overlapping stitches achieve different degrees of color and texture.

Figure 4-12. Framed stitchery by Carlos Cobos (15" × 15"). Satin stitches form solid rows along edges of applied ribbons. Linear shapes overlay each other. (Courtesy, James Yaw Gallery)

Monograms or Names: Project

Try your (or someone else's) monogram or name. Any type of lettering can be used—block or script, upper or lower case. Suggested lettering styles are shown in Figure 4-15. (Automatic monogram attachments are available for some machines.) Letters can form the basis of a design, or they can become the subject of an entire piece.

Draw the design on paper or directly on the fabric, using tailors' chalk so that any errors can be easily rubbed out. If the design is on paper, pin it to the face of the fabric. If the design is drawn on the fabric, back the fabric with paper to reinforce it or stretch tightly in a hoop.

Practice first on scrap fabric and with the same paper or hoop setup you plan to use for the project. Position the setup under the needle, bring the bobbin thread up through the fabric, and lock both threads in place. Gently guide the fabric, or hoop, to follow the contours of the letters, and sew as if drawing with a pencil. Practice stitching the loops, lines, curves, and circles that form the different parts of letters.

To stitch letters in script, set the machine for the desired width, and test the stitching to adjust the length. You can shade the stitch lines by making some wide and others thin as in the example, "Gary" (Figure 4-14). Note that the downstrokes in the example are wide, while the upstrokes and cross strokes are narrow. To vary the stitches evenly as you move from one width to another, guide the fabric with your left hand while turning the stitch width control with your right. If this is too difficult to do at first, stitch slowly and stop whenever you have to adjust the width. Better control is achieved at a slower speed.

When the lettering is completed, cut or gently tear away the paper. You may find that the needle per-forations have already cut the paper loose in many places, so all you may have to do is clip a few uncut pieces. A seam ripper is a handy tool to use when prying up those little pieces. Pull thread ends through to the reverse side and tie them for a neat ending.

To make letters in a consistent width throughout (see "Carolyn" in Figure 4-14), draw the design, prepare fabric, and adjust settings as before. As always, practice first. To turn round corners (in letters such as *a, c, d, e, o*), keep stitches at an equal distance from the center of the circle or partial circle. You may find that the stitches start to angle as you turn for these round corners. The best way to avoid this, and to achieve a more perfect roundness, is to use a circle guide (see Stitching Circles). When stitching with the guide, be careful to maintain the same number of stitches per inch throughout.

Letters can also be made with free motion satin stitches. A circle guide is not necessary for this.

Figure 4-13. Satin-stitching monogram through paper which is removed upon completion. Monogram can also be drawn directly on fabric.

Figure 4-14. Two examples of satin-stitched monograms.

Figure 4-15. Lettering styles.

In cutwork, sometimes called open work, webbed designs are formed by stitching across holes cut in the fabric. The holes can be different sizes and shapes and can be backed with contrasting fabrics. When the cutwork is applied to a background, such as a wall, table-top, or window, the pattern and color of that background will become part of the design. These airy, open pieces can be further enhanced by using various embroidery stitches. (In another type of cutwork—reverse applique, the fabric is layered, with sections of the top layers cut away to form the design.)

Plan a design suitable for cutwork. Draw it on typing paper or directly onto the face side of the fabric. (Or draw a reverse design and work from the back—see Transferring Designs—then you will not have to remove every small bit of paper from the stitching. However, keep in mind that the worst results of unbalanced stitching will show on the face.) If the design is on paper, pin the paper to the fabric. If it is on the fabric, back fabric with paper to prevent puckering. Stretch the fabric firmly in a hoop and position it under the needle. Bring the bobbin thread through and lock both threads in place.

Set your machine for narrow zig-zag stitch, and stitch the main lines of the design; this establishes the guidelines for the next stitches. If you drew the design on paper, cut or tear the paper away at this point. Reset the machine to a stitch of your choice, and stitch over the lines. (Mostly satin stitch was used as the outline in the example shown in Figure 4-16.) On the edges that will contain the cutwork, use a narrow to medium width zigzag or satin stitch.

Remove the hoop from under the needle, and cut or tear away any

Figure 4-16. Stitch outline of design.

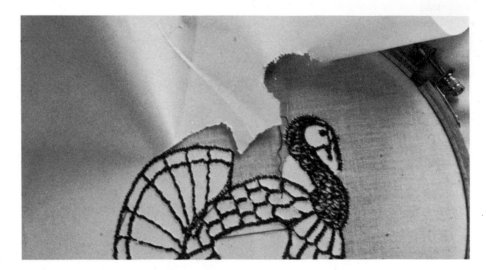

Figure 4-17. Cut away paper backing from reverse side.

Figure 4-18. Remove paper from enclosed areas with seam ripper.

46

paper backing. Use a seam ripper to pry up any stubborn pieces. Then carefully cut away the fabric from the areas that will contain the cutwork. Use small, sharp scissors and cut close to the stitching. Do all this while the design remains in the hoop. Only if the design is too large to be contained within the hoop area would you remove it. It is also easier to cut fabric while it is held taut in a hoop.

Replace the hoop under the needle. Lock stitches in place on the edge of an open area and stitch across the area, moving the hoop freely with your hands as you go. Stitch slowly at first to see if your machine will stitch across the cut out spaces. The needle thread will twist around the bobbin thread. How tightly these stitches intertwine will depend on how fast you stitch and move the hoop.

When you get to the opposite edge, lock stitches in place and stitch along the edge to the next crossing point. Stitch across the opening to form another line in the design. Continue in this fashion until you have stitched a number of lines that go in one direction. Bisect these lines with other lines, locking stitches at the beginning and end of each line. The first set of stitches will furnish a base for those that follow. You can vary the stitching by making a spoked pattern, or a network of lines traveling in various directions, or an asymmetrical, freely stitched invention.

Threads can also be linked to form a lacelike design. In the cutwork turkey (Figure 4-20), the thread down the center of each tail feather forms a base for the threads that

cross (also see Figure 4-19). When changing direction, link the crossing and center threads. To do this, stitch across to the center thread and catch it with the crossing thread. If it will not catch, stitch another thread down the center, parallel to the first, in order to give the crossing thread two threads to catch.

When all the lines of your design have been completed, remove the fabric from the hoop and back it with paper. Reposition the fabric in the hoop, stretching it tightly again, and place it under the needle. Outline all the cutwork areas with a satin stitch that is wider than the edge it is to cover. This second layer of stitches adds firmness to the edge and makes it neat by covering any loose threads. In the cutwork turkey, a wide zigzag stitch was also used to give a fuzzy, feathery look to the edges.

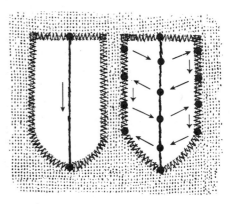

Figure 4-19. (*Left*) Stitch a line down center of cutout shape to form base for crossing stitches. (*Right*) To change direction, stitch to center line, catch the line, change direction, and stitch to opposite edge.

Figure 4-20. Cutwork turkey by Carolyn Hall (4″ × 4″). Fabric cut away from some areas; cutwork designs in center of turkey and in tail feathers.

FREE MOTION STITCHING

This technique is a popular means of achieving an artistic effect quickly. By eliminating the action of the feed and reducing pressure on the presser foot, stitches can move in any direction as freely as a drawn line meandering on a page. (There is no need to turn the fabric. To make a circle, for example, sew as if drawing with a pencil.) The many exciting design possibilities in this type of stitching will become obvious once you begin to experiment. To learn the rhythm of free embroidery, all you need is a good supply of fabric on which to practice.

On some sewing machines, the feed dogs have to be lowered or else covered with a metal plate to allow free movement of the fabric. Consult your manual to see what is recommended for your machine. Many stitchers have found that setting the stitch length at 0 is sufficient to eliminate feed dog movement. No other adjustment may be necessary for your machine.

For greater visibility while stitching, use a clear plastic zigzag presser foot, if you have one; if not, a metal one will do. For those who have straight stitch machines, the straight stitch foot can also be used for free motion sewing. Release presser foot pressure to the lightest or "darn" setting. Enough pressure will still be exerted to keep the fabric in contact with the needle plate so that no stitches are skipped. If your machine does not have this setting, use a darning foot (or darning spring) instead. It will hold the fabric in place while a stitch is being made and release it for free motion movement between the stitches. Even the oldest sewing machines can free sew if darning attachments that fit them can be found.

Set the machine for a balanced stitch. Use a fairly stiff fabric at the beginning; soft fabrics will have to be reinforced. Draw the bobbin thread through the fabric and lock the ends in place. For free motion embroidery, use your hands to keep the fabric flat. Place them a couple of inches apart on each side of the needle, enclosing the area to be sewn as if with a hoop, and pulling the fab-

Figure 4-21. *Eight Faces* by Claudia Hall (6" × 12"). An experiment in free motion stitching. Features are stitched in continuous lines to avoid an excess of thread ends.

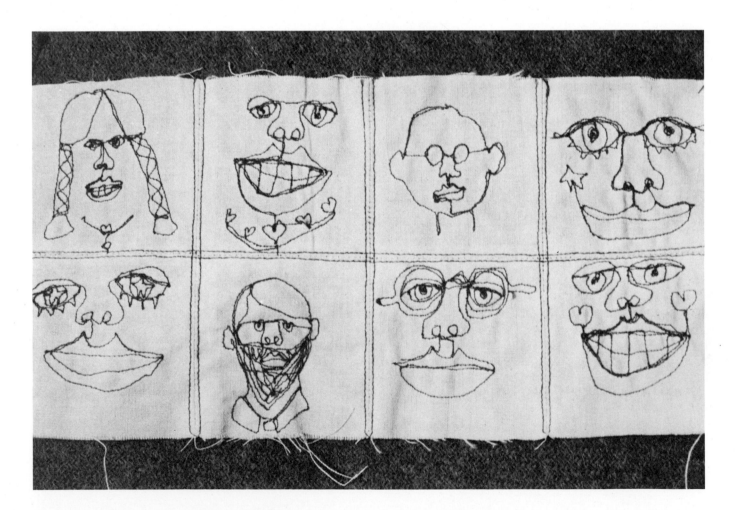

ric taut. This takes some practice, but your hands are really your best tools.

Because fabric movement is no longer controlled by the feed, stitch size will depend on how slowly or rapidly you move the fabric. The slower you move it, the smaller the stitch; the faster you move it, the larger the stitch. For a smooth line, stitch very rapidly and move the fabric slowly. Take care not to pull the fabric against the needle while the stitch is being formed (particularly if you are not using a darning foot), or the thread or needle may break.

Move the fabric freely in any direction: forward, backward, to the left, to the right. Stitch straight lines, circles, spirals, curves. Overlap stitch lines when it pleases you to do so. Develop a rhythm as you stitch. Try sewing over stitches to create different textural qualities and to build up the design. As soon as you gain confidence in your ability to control the machine, try stitching some simple shapes, then more complicated ones. For increased interest, use various fabrics of different weights. The free motion technique is also ideal for making lettering designs (Figure 4-23) and for outlining quilting designs, since there is no need to turn the fabric to follow the pattern.

When a design is completed, lock the ends in place. If the design rambles on in one long, continuous line, you will have fewer ends to contend with. If you use heavy thread, leave the ends long enough to be inserted in a sewing needle, worked to the back, and fastened.

Free motion embroidery can be worked with or without a hoop. Stiff fabrics usually do not require a hoop,

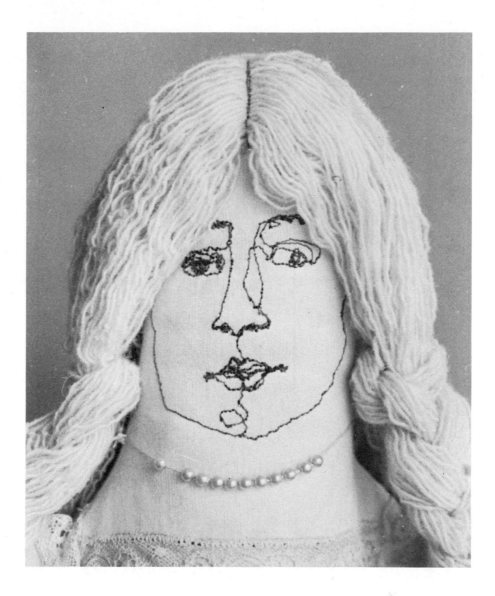

but some stitchers prefer to use one anyway. Lightweight fabrics, or those that pucker easily, are more conveniently handled when enclosed tightly in a hoop or when stiffened; use both methods if fabric pulls up on each upstroke of the needle. Free motion embroidery can also be worked without a presser foot.

Figure 4-22. Closeup of *Muslin Lady* by Carolyn Hall shows application of free motion stitching on a stuffed figure.

Figure 4-23. Suggested lettering style.

abcdefghijklmnopqrstuvwxyz

Free Motion Satin Stitch

This technique nearly always requires a hoop, since the stitch pulls the fabric and will cause all but the stiffest to pucker. As with any stitch in free motion embroidery, you can work with or without a presser foot. *Note:* When working without a presser foot, be extremely careful to keep your fingers away from the needle. Also, be sure to lower the presser foot lever; top thread tension is not engaged when the lever is up.

Try this.... Trace a design or sketch it freehand onto the face side of the fabric. A design does not have to be complicated to be artistically effective; one built of simple shapes, particularly abstract shapes, is just as successful. Center the design in an embroidery hoop. Stretch the fabric so it is taut and the grain lines run straight all the way across.

Set the machine for free motion embroidery and for zigzag stitch. Remove the presser foot. Use embroidery thread in the needle, darning thread in the bobbin. Slide the hoop under the needle. *Lower the presser foot lever.* Bring the bobbin thread through the fabric and lock the ends in place.

Hold the hoop, encircling it with your fingers, thumbs at the front and nearly touching. You may have to use your forefingers to press the fabric flat against the needle plate; if the fabric is not held flat, the needle will not pick up the bobbin thread. Run the machine at an even speed, following the contours of the design shapes. Once the shapes are outlined, fill them in. Overlap the stitches for solid areas or work in adjacent rows, if you prefer. Control the direction and speed of fabric movement by guiding the hoop with both hands, drawing with it as you would a pencil. Stitch with the grain to diminish the possibility of puckering. If you use two or more colors, try to plan the order of your stitching to avoid constant rethreading of the machine for each color change. Even though satin stitch is a slightly unbalanced stitch and therefore best worked from the face side of the fabric, any stitches used with it can be worked from either side, provided their tensions are not also altered.

Figure 4-24. Work in progress by Carolyn Hall. Free motion stitches tend to pucker fabric, even though held in a hoop and backed with paper. To "take-up" puckering, the background (partially done) will be completely covered with bobbin thread couching worked from the reverse side.

Altered Tension Stitches

The samplers in Figures 4-25 and 4-26 show some of the results of altered ("couched") stitches in free motion embroidery. Read both the *Needle Thread Sampler* and the *Bobbin Thread Sampler* from top to bottom. With a heavier thread in the bobbin, obtain a balanced stitch, then reduce pressure on the presser foot or otherwise prepare the machine for free motion embroidery. on the presser foot or otherwise prepare the machine for free motion embroidery.

Needle Thread Sampler

Tighten top tension until the bobbin thread comes through to couch the needle thread. If you cannot increase tension sufficiently, try loosening bobbin tension or bypassing the tension spring. Next straight stitch a row of loops joined together **(Row 1)**. The tight top thread pulls the bobbin thread up into long couching stitches. An even greater pull is exerted by the top thread when a turn is made to form a loop. Make some "daisy stitch" loops, then try a row of zigzag for a "feather stitch" **(Row 5)**.

Bobbin Thread Sampler

You will not be able to see the couching stitches being formed, since you will be working on the face side and they will appear on the back. The sampler shows the back of the fabric. Loosen top tension until the top thread loops around the bobbin thread. Straight stitch a row of "daisy stitch" **(Row 1)**. The tighter bobbin thread will pull the loose top thread into long couching stitches. Loosen top tension for still longer couching stitches. Try smaller loops **(Row 2)**, closer together. Progressively tighten top tension for **Rows 3, 4, and 5,** and make loops larger in each row. In **Row 6,** regular thread was used in the bobbin.

Figure 4-25. Needle thread sampler.

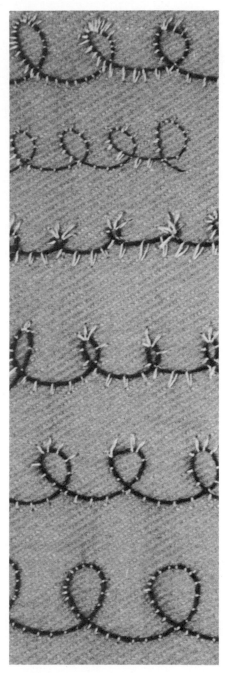

Figure 4-26. Bobbin thread sampler.

Note: When you remove the piece from the machine, hold the last stitch down with your finger and pull the fabric gently to one side to clip the threads. Otherwise, the threads will draw up in the fabric, causing it to pucker.

Denim Tote: Project

Finished size: Approximately 19 by 12 inches (48.3 by 30.5 cm).

Materials: Blue denim fabric, 2/3 yard (66 cm), 36 inches (9.1 cm) wide; lining (your choice), 19 by 26 inches (48.3 by 66 cm); padding (polyester batting or soft, thick fabric), 21 by 26 inches (53.3 by 66 cm); rope, 12 feet (3.6m) long.

Technique: Free motion and straight stitch. Darning foot for free motion sewing (or use straight stitch or zigzag foot and ease presser foot pressure). You will probably not need a hoop if you hold the fabric down and encircle the stitching with your hands.

Directions (refer to Figure 4-29 throughout). Join all pieces with ⅝ inch (1.6 cm) seams, unless stated otherwise; seam allowances are included in dimensions given. Measure and cut denim to its working size of 21 by 26 inches (53.3 by 66 cm). From the remainder, measure and cut two tabs, each 6 by 4 inches (15.2 by 10.2 cm). Decide on a design and sketch it onto the face of the denim (use tailors' chalk or a chalk pencil), or plan to stitch spontaneously.

Pin padding to the wrong side of the denim and machine baste in place. Set the machine for free motion embroidery. Use heavy thread in the needle (if the heavy thread gives problems, use two regular threads) and loosen the top thread tension. Place pins at intervals over the denim face. Stitch the design at an even pace, using only as much speed as you can handle.

Once the design is completed, begin assembling the tote. Fold each tab lengthwise, edges meeting in the center. Fold lengthwise again to conceal cut edges. Each tab should now measure 6 by 1 inch (15.2 by 2.5 cm). Stitch lengthwise edges together; seams should be narrow. Fold one tab in half to form a loop. Pin it so that its raw edges meet the top edge of the denim and the loop ends lay flat on the denim face. Pin the other tab 5 inches (12.7 cm) down from the top edge in the same manner.

Pin the lining to the denim, right sides facing, top edges meeting. Note that the lining is 2 inches (5.1 cm) shorter than the denim. Set the machine for straight stitch and thread the needle with regular thread. Sew lining, denim, and padding together across their top edges (the top loop will be stitched into this seam).

Lay lining and denim flat, right sides up. Fold lengthwise, right sides facing, side edges matching. Begin stitching 2 inches (5.1 cm) up from the bottom denim edge and on the fold. Make a rounded corner, stitch across the bottom; make a rounded corner, stitch up the side across the pinned loop, and onto the lining; make another rounded corner and stop 2 inches (5.1 cm) from the corner. Leave an 8 to 9 inch (20 to 22 cm) opening for turning. Begin stitching again 2 inches (5.1 cm) from the fold, make a rounded corner and end off.

Trim seams and turn the tote right-side out. Turn the edges of the opening under, and stitch closed. Push the lining into the tote; this leaves an inside denim hem of about 1¼ inches (3 cm). Topstitch through all three layers at the base of the top seam. Reinforce the seam of the top loop.

Cut rope in half to make two 6-foot (1.8m) lengths. Thread two ends through the top loop and braid the resulting four strands together. Thread braid ends through the side loop and tie a knot to secure.

Figure 4-27. *(Front view)* Denim tote (approximately 19″ × 12″). Note braid ends threaded and knotted through side loop.

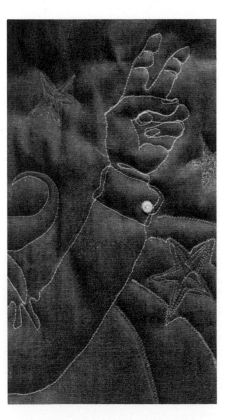

Figure 4-28. *(Back view)* Design lines freely stitched in two strands of regular thread on blue denim.

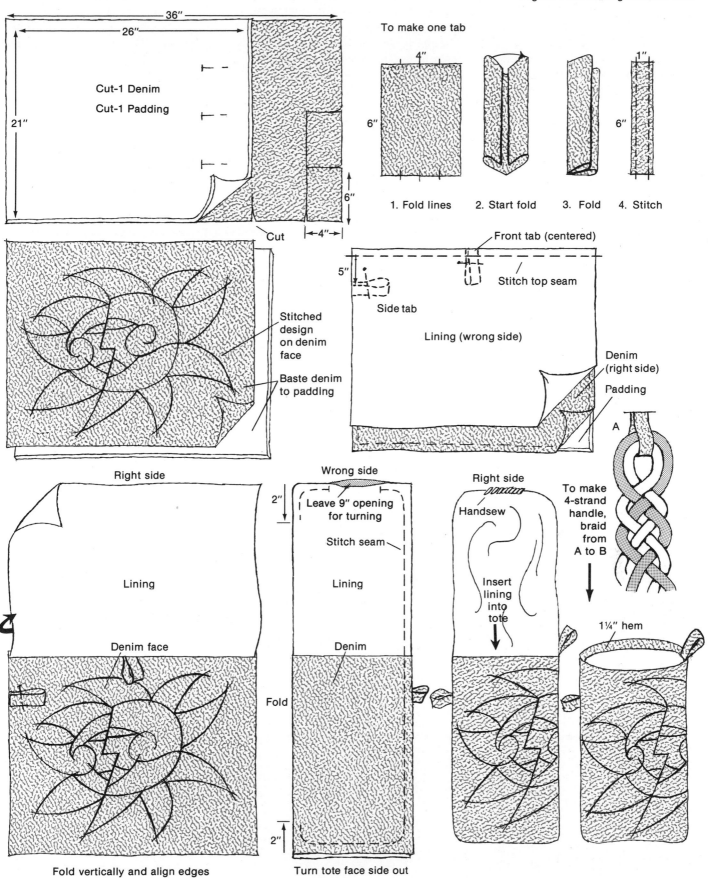

Figure 4-29. Making a denim tote.

36″

26″

Cut-1 Denim

Cut-1 Padding

21″

6″

Cut

|←4″→|

To make one tab

4″

6″

6″

1″

1. Fold lines   2. Start fold   3. Fold   4. Stitch

Stitched design on denim face

Baste denim to padding

Front tab (centered)

5″

Side tab

Stitch top seam

Lining (wrong side)

Denim (right side)

Padding

A

Right side

Lining

Denim face

Fold vertically and align edges

Wrong side

2″

Leave 9″ opening for turning

Stitch seam

Lining

Denim

Fold

2″

Turn tote face side out

Right side

Handsew

Insert lining into tote

To make 4-strand handle, braid from A to B

1¼″ hem

AUTOMATIC DECORATIVE STITCHES

Now for the sewing machine's virtuoso performance—the automatic decorative stitches. Some automatic patterns expand the range of decorative machine embroidery, while others are just for fun, like the Scottie dog stitch or the tulip stitch. The formation of automatic stitches is controlled by cams (stitch pattern discs) which are built into some machines, or which are insertable, or both. These cams enable the machine to simulate almost any hand embroidery stitch. This does not mean that machine embroidery is in competition with hand embroidery; each has special and unique qualities. Often both techniques can be incorporated effectively in a single piece.

Because of the regularity of the automatic stitches, their potential has not been fully explored by those textile artists who consider regularity to be monotonous. But innovative stitchers, who are more patient in their experimenting, have learned to control the patterns to achieve variety and charm.

Although the stitch patterns are usually used decoratively, they also serve a practical purpose. They can finish a raw edge, top stitch a seam, emphasize a line, and highlight or outline an area. Shapes can be filled in by using one stitch pattern throughout or by combining several in the same design. Filling stitches can be placed close together or spaced apart for a more open feeling. Pattern units can be combined separately to make other motifs.

To familiarize yourself with this technique, experiment on a stiff fabric or use a hoop. Use a zigzag presser foot or special-purpose foot. Machine settings are essentially the same as for satin stitching, but consult your manual for specific recommendations.

Practice turning a square corner to see how the stitches should be placed. Some patterns are several stitches long and might look best if completed before the corner is turned. However, if a pattern varies from a wide to a narrow width, it is best to make the turn on the wide part of a stitch. Make the turn as in zigzag stitching (Figure 4-7, Row 8), with the needle inserted on the side opposite to the direction of the turn so that you will stitch over the previous stitches rather than make an open corner and leave a gap.

If you are making a rectangular shape and want the patterns on the opposite sides to match perfectly, or if you are making parallel rows, you may have to gently push or pull the fabric on the return trip, placing your fingers on either side of the pattern as you stitch. When stitching curves, guide the fabric slowly as it

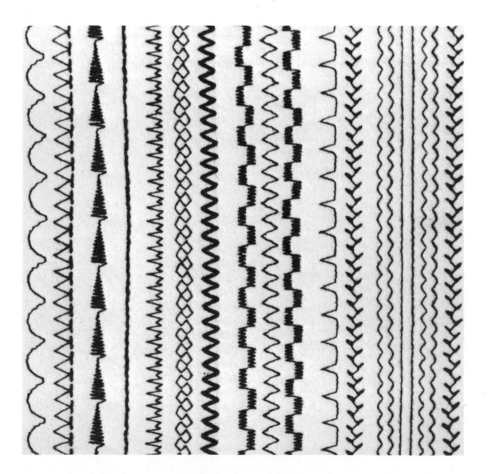

Figure 4-30. Examples of automatic decorative stitches. (Courtesy, The Singer Company)

turns so that the pattern maintains its shape. Watch the formation of the stitches through the slot in the presser foot.

Variations in the design can occur by varying the width and/or length of a stitch but, here again, consult your manual to see if a particular pattern can be so modified. Additional variations can be achieved by trying threads of different types and colors. Still further variations are possible if twin or triple needles are used—thread them in contrasting colors for a shadow effect.

Try These ....

1. Sketch a simple shape—a circle, a square, a garden fence, or an animal. Outline and fill in the shape with automatic stitches, or use satin stitch or any decorative stitch for outlining. The filling stitches can follow the contours of the shape, can overlap them, or meet them at random. If you prefer an orderly design, make the rows geometrically precise. Any of these approaches can be made aesthetically satisfying through the use of color and/or the emphasis on certain stitches and their placement.

2. Stitch ribbons or cutout shapes onto a background. A row of "darts" down the center of a ribbon with a row of scallops on its edges can produce a handsome result. The ribbons or shapes could also be stitched separately and then applied to a background fabric.

3. Combine pattern stitches with other techniques. Whatever can be accomplished with zigzag stitching may also be possible with the pattern stitches; this includes couching heavy or decorative threads. Take advantage of the free motion techniques (see Figure 4-31). The combination of the machine busily pounding out its pattern and you moving the fabric freely can produce delightful results.

Figure 4-31. Sampler by Carolyn Hall (7" × 10"). Automatic stitches, using the free motion technique, outline as well as fill in the shape.

5. COUCHING

Figure 5-1. Machine couched decorations on felt Peruvian hat. (Courtesy, Arlen Linn)

Couching permits the use of yarns and threads too heavy, stiff, or fragile to be threaded through the machine or sewn through the fabric. Instead, they are laid onto the fabric surface and are fastened down with stitches. Any material that the needle can go through or around can be couched in place. This includes rug yarn, various cords and twines, ribbon, raffia, grasses, small twigs, pipe

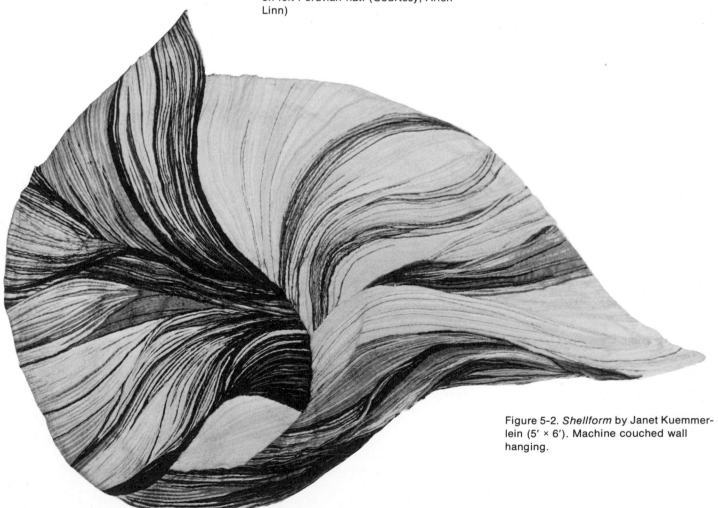

Figure 5-2. *Shellform* by Janet Kuemmerlein (5' × 6'). Machine couched wall hanging.

56

cleaners, buttons, and beads. (For demonstration purposes, yarn is used in the samplers in this section.) You can also crochet a chain, tie a series of knots, or braid any number of strands to be laid on the fabric and couched. In addition, a variety of machine stitches can be used: straight, zigzag, blind hem, or decorative.

EMBROIDERY COUCHING

Embroidery couching can be worked in several ways, depending on the effect you are striving for, the materials you are using, and what your machine can (or prefers) to do:

1. With a presser foot, using regular or reduced pressure.

2. Without a presser foot, but with a hoop to keep the fabric taut, or without a presser foot or hoop. Paper or other stiffening can be used to back the fabric.

These methods are illustrated in the samplers that follow.

Couching with Presser Foot

Couching Sampler

The sampler in Figure 5-3 shows several examples of embroidery couching. Work the rows with the special-purpose foot, if you have one; if not, you may have a cording foot (it has a slot for insertion of yarn or cord), or a buttonhole foot which has the cording device built in. Lacking these, use the zigzag or straight stitch foot and ease presser foot pressure. The reason for this careful selection is to keep the yarn, especially wool yarn, from stretching while being couched, causing the fabric to curl or pucker.

Unless suggested otherwise, thread the needle with a matching or contrasting color, or with clear nylon thread for nearly invisible stitches. Check drapery or upholstery stores for the clear nylon thread and buy the "fine" size. This thread is very

stiff, so be careful that it does not unwind or tangle. Thread the bobbin with darning thread or regular thread.

Draw a series of straight, parallel lines on a firm fabric. Place the yarn between the presser foot toes, or into the slot of the cording or buttonhole foot. Begin each row by stitching one end of the yarn in place on the fabric. While stitching, guide the yarn by hand so it follows along the lines, but be careful not to pull it.

Row 1. Satin Stitch Couching. Set the machine for medium to wide satin stitch. Use any thread that will stitch through your needle (from regular or decorative thread to yarn), and in a color matching the yarn to be couched. A cording (or buttonhole) foot is an advantage in this row and the next since it keeps the yarn centered, leaving you free to concentrate on following the lines. If you are not satisfied with the row when finished, go over it with a fractionally wider satin stitch.

Row 2. Straight Stitch Couching. Set the machine for straight stitch, 12 to 15 stitches per inch (2.5 cm), or less if you prefer. *Note:* If you cannot

ease presser foot pressure sufficiently and have no cording foot, you may find it easier to couch this row without a presser foot (see next two samplers).

Row 3. Altered Bobbin Thread Tension. For comparison, a row of bobbin thread couching stitched from the reverse side is included. The heavy thread is in the bobbin.

Row 4. Zigzag Stitch Couching. Set the machine for wide zigzag, 6 or more stitches per inch. This type of couching is most suited to long, continuous rows. Make stitches at various widths and lengths to achieve the spaced intervals you prefer.

Row 5. Same as Row 4, except that the couched yarn is a rayon slub.

Row 6. Blind Hem Stitch Couching. Since the yarn is caught just on one side by the occasional zigzag in this stitch, its characteristics are allowed to show clearly. If your machine does not have a blind hem setting, approximate the stitch by making a few straight stitches, then a zigzag, and repeat. Hand turn the wheel for the zigzag if you have no zigzag setting. Use long or short stitches.

Figure 5-3. Couching sampler.

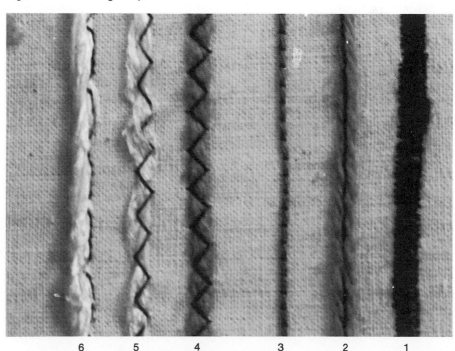

6   5   4   3   2   1

Couching without Presser Foot

When working in this manner, you can change direction whenever your design calls for it, or you can catch the yarn with a few stitches at certain points only.

Zinnia Sampler

In this sampler, the stitches catch the looped yarn at the edges. This allows the loops to rise freely from the fabric. Many stitchers use this technique to make machine-sewn versions of hand-embroidery stitches such as lazy daisy, feather stitch, French knots, and others. The yarns are laid in place to simulate the stitch and are couched down. For a charm-ing use of this technique, sew patches of colored fabrics onto a background and overlay with couched yarns.

You can work with or without a hoop. If you do not use a hoop, back the fabric with paper to keep it firm. Since yarn designs work up quickly, requiring the fabric to be moved often, working without a hoop is an advantage—unless, of course, the hoop encloses the entire design. However, if you cannot make this technique work on your fabric without a hoop then, by all means, use one.

Set the machine for straight stitch. Use clear nylon or matching thread in the needle; darning or regular thread in the bobbin. For the yarn, use one, two, or more colors throughout. You will also need a pair of long tweezers to hold the fabric against the needle plate—and to keep from stitching your fingers together.

You work very close to the needle in this technique, *so be careful.* Guide the fabric with one hand, and hold the tweezers against the fabric with the other.

Draw two circles on the fabric, one inside the other. Lower the presser foot lever, place one yarn end on the outer circle and lock it in place. Loop the yarn and stitch it down along its inside edges (Figure 5-5). Continue making loops and stitching them down in this fashion until the outer circle is filled in. Then move to the inner circle and repeat (Figure 5-6). Continue making loops until a small area is left in the center of the shape. Make a series of knots in the yarn, and fill in the center (Figure 5-7). Instead of the knots, you can make tiny loops or whatever else you prefer. At completion, cut the thread and yarn off close to the surface, or insert the yarn in a tapestry needle, pull it to the underside, and cut it off.

Figure 5-5. Zinnia sampler. Loop yarn and stitch its inside edges around rim of outer circle. Use tweezers to hold fabric against needle plate. Work with or without hoop.

Figure 5-6. Outer circle completed; repeat for inner circle. Note tweezers holding yarn in place.

Figure 5-7. Inner circle completed. Fill in center by knotting yarn and stitching it down.

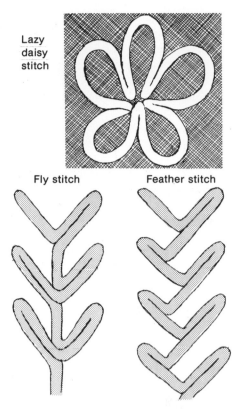

Lazy daisy stitch

Fly stitch   Feather stitch

Figure 5-4. Examples of hand embroidery stitches that can be simulated on the sewing machine.

Satin Stitch Sampler

In this technique, yarn is laid in closely spaced rows so that it resembles satin stitch in crewel embroidery. The resemblance is created by stitching across a shape, stopping with the needle inserted on a line, bringing the yarn across to the line, and anchoring it with one or two stitches. This is repeated until the shape is filled in. In order to stop the needle exactly where you want it, keep your right hand on the handwheel and turn it manually for the last few stitches. Both moving the hoop and manipulating the yarn will be done mostly with your left hand. This is one of those techniques that are really easy to do, but that seems to require three hands while doing them.

Set the machine for straight stitch. Use darning or regular thread in the bobbin, and clear nylon thread, if you have it, in the needle (if not, use a matching color). You will also need a hoop and tweezers.

Draw the shape outlines on the fabric—either the flower design shown or one of your choice. When designing for this technique, analyze the shapes in terms of straight lines, arranging the lines in whatever directions are necessary to follow the pattern. To guide the stitching, draw the directional lines on the fabric.

Stretch the fabric in the hoop. Slide the hoop under the needle, and lower the presser foot lever. Begin by placing the yarn end inside the shape where it will eventually be covered by an overlapping row. For example, place it at the tip of a shape (Figure 5-8, *A*), or at the midpoint of a line. Secure the end with a bar tack. Keep the yarn out of the way of the needle, and stitch across the shape to where the yarn will be anchored next. In this sampler, it is brought to the outline (Figure 5-8, *B*). Stop with the needle inserted on the edge. Bring the yarn across (as it doubles over itself, it will cover the yarn end), and anchor it in place with

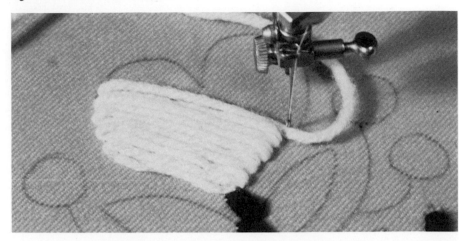

Figure 5-9. Satin stitch sampler.

(*A*) Partially completed design. Secure yarn with stitches at end of line.

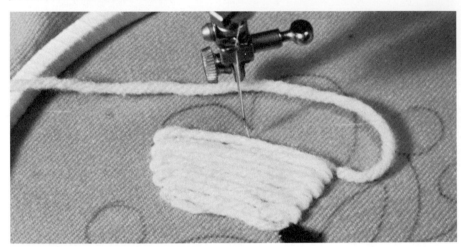

(*B*) Stitch across shape as close to previously laid row as possible. Keep yarn out of way of stitches.

(*C*) Bring yarn across, position it against previous row. Tweezers help hold yarn in place for anchoring.

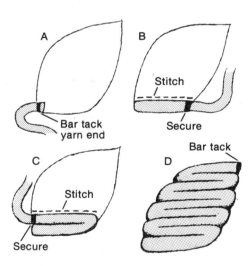

Figure 5-8. Leaf couched to simulate satin stitch in hand embroidery. (*A*) Secure yarn end. (*B*) Stitch across leaf, bring yarn across, tack it down. (*C*) Stitch to opposite side, bring yarn across, covering previous stitch line and yarn end. (*D*) Continue stitching and bring yarn across to complete leaf.

one or two stitches (Figure 5-8, *C*).

Stitch back across the shape, as closely as possible to the laid yarn and parallel with it. Stop with the needle inserted on the outline and next to the place where it was anchored. Bring the yarn across (it will cover the row of stitches just made) and anchor it in place (Figure 5-8, *D*). Continue in this fashion until one leaf is filled in.

At the finish, lock the yarn end with a bar tack, and cut off close to the surface. Then move to the next shape. Whenever possible, plan your design so that the cut-off end of one shape will be covered by overlapping yarns in the next shape. For example, couch the leaves so they end at the stem, then couch the stem to overlap the endings (see Figure 5-9, *D*).

In certain areas of the sampler, yarns were couched with straight stitches—in the small stems, along the edges of the leaves, and around the coiled outlines of the buds.

With these couching techniques, you can arrange the yarns in a simulated version of nearly every hand embroidery stitch.

(*D*) Completed sampler. Note coiled outlines of buds and straight stitch couching along edges of leaves.

FLOSSA

In this method, a fringe is produced by winding yarn (or other fibers or fabric) around a frame and stitching down its center. The fringe is stitched either directly onto a background fabric, or stitched and applied afterward (to a woven, knitted or crocheted background). Either way, a pile results that closely resembles the flossa pile in weaving. Various colors and textures can be combined in one flossa strip. Loops can be of different heights, the pile cut or uncut. Further interest can be provided by stitching one flossa row over another.

Machine flossa works up quickly, is sturdy, and can be used to fashion rugs, afghans, wall hangings, pillow covers, muffs, and stoles; other possibilities will occur to you once you become involved with the technique.

Flossa Frame. You need a U-shaped frame to wind the yarn around and to support it for stitching. The frame can be a wire coat hanger bent to shape, cardboard cut to shape, a Tinker Toy fitted to shape (it works), or a hairpin crochet loom

(Figure 5-10). Make the frame twice the width of the planned flossa fringe (when yarns are stitched down the center, two flossa rows are formed).

Draw guidelines on the background fabric; these will be covered by the sewn flossa. Use a ruler for straight lines, or plan circular or curved lines. If the yarn will be stitched directly onto the fabric, straight lines will be the easiest to follow; if the flossa will be stitched and then applied, any shape lines can be drawn.

Setting. Set the machine for short straight stitch or small zigzag. Cotton-wrapped polyester thread in both the needle and bobbin will hold the yarn firmly to the fabric. Use a zigzag presser foot. If the presser foot toes get caught in the yarn, place masking tape across them at the front; or use a quilting foot, zipper foot, or darning foot. Another way is to lay a strip of paper, about 1 inch (2.5 cm) wide, on the yarn; remove the paper when stitching is finished.

Stitching a Flossa Row. Wind yarn evenly around the frame, not so loosely that it sags and not so tightly that it pulls the frame inward. It should slide easily on the frame. Wind from the open end to the closed

end, until there is just enough yarn to make 3 to 4 inches (7.6 to 10.2 cm) of flossa at a time; more than this could be unwieldy. You can work with a continuous length or with short lengths.

Place the wound frame on the machine with its open end away from you. Center it on a stitch line so there is an equal amount of yarn on each side. Lock the first stitches on the seam allowance, or at least ½ inch (1.3 cm) from where the yarn will be stitched down. Then stitch along the center of the frame, from its open end to its closed end, until the wound yarn is stitched in place. Stop with the needle inserted in the fabric, and pull the frame carefully toward you, slipping off most of the sewn loops as you do so. Rewind the frame and resume stitching. Repeat this process for each row (Figure 5-11).

If you want the loops cut, do so after completing each row. Or cut them while they are still on the frame by sliding scissors along the outside edges.

If you are sewing the flossa fringe separately, stitch along the center of the yarn with the paper strip in place. Remove the paper and apply the fringe to your planned project.

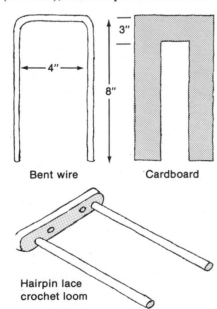

Figure 5-10. Homemade flossa frame. Yarn is wound around frame and stitched to make a fringe.

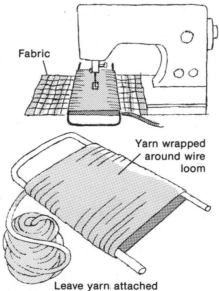

Figure 5-11. Wind yarn evenly around frame from open to closed end, then stitch down the center onto background fabric.

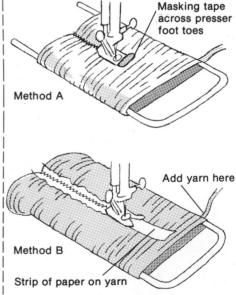

Figure 5-12. If presser foot toes catch in yarn, use tape or a strip of paper. Also use strip when making a separate fringe.

Flossa Pillow: Project

Finished Size. 12 by 14 inches (30.5 by 35.6 cm), excluding tassels.

Materials: 4-ply knitting worsted, 4-oz. (114g) each; blue-purple (A), red (B), orange (C), bright pink (D), or colors related to background fabric. Nubby weave upholstery fabric or a handweave, 14 by 32 inches (35.6 by 81.3 cm). Purchased pillow or polyester fiberfill stuffing (make a pillow case to contain stuffing if you wish). Flossa frame, 4 inches (10.2 cm) wide for a 2 inch (5.1 cm) pile.

Technique: Refer to the beginning of this section for settings and instructions on making a frame.

Directions: Cut two pieces of fabric, each 14 by 16 inches (35.6 by 40.6 cm), for front and back. This includes 1 inch (2.5 cm) seam allowances. On the face fabric, draw or stitch parallel, lengthwise lines starting and ending 1 inch (2.5 cm) from each edge and at these intervals: 1, 5, 3, 3, and 2 inches (2.5, 12.7, 7.6, 7.6, and 5.1 cm) (see Figure 5-13).

Wind color A around the frame. Slide yarn close enough together to have 18 windings (or loops) per inch (cm). Wind fairly loosely, since wool yarn seems to tighten as more is added. Center the frame on row 1. Lock the first stitches on the seamline, and begin stitching the yarn down on the drawn line. Continue stitching sections of yarn in place, winding on more yarn as needed, until you have completed a row. Lock the last stitches, and cut the loops.

Work the next three rows in the same manner, and in these colors: C and D for row 2; B and C for row 3; B, C, and D for row 4. On these rows, cut loops on one side only (see Figure 5-13).

Tassels. Cut a piece of cardboard, 8 inches (20.3 cm) long. Wind A around it 40 times. Insert a doubled yarn strand through one end of the wound yarn, and tie into a tight knot. Cut yarn off the cardboard at the

other end. Wrap B and C 1½ inches (3.8 cm) down from the tied end and 4 times around. Pull very tightly and knot. Let these ends mingle with the tassel strands. Make 8 tassels in all. Then make 8 tassels with B and C, and wrap with A and D for a total of 16 tassels, each about 6 inches (15.2 cm) long.

To attach tassels, turn the pillow cover face up, and lay tassels on the lengthwise edges with wrapped ends on the seamlines and open ends on

the fabric face. Place backing over, face down. Stitch tassels and lengthwise edges together. Then stitch widthwise edges together, leaving an opening for turning—6 inches (15.2 cm) for stuffing, more for the pillow. Trim corners, turn the cover rightside out, and stuff. Turn edges of the opening under and slipstitch closed.

Note: if you wish, sew flossa rows separately, then apply to the pillow face.

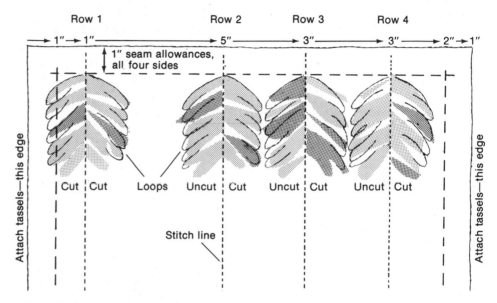

Figure 5-13. Pattern for flossa pillow.

Figure 5-14. Flossa pillow (12″ × 14″, excluding tassels).

Fur and Flossa Pillow: Project

The finished pillow is 14 inches (35.6 cm) square, but the long pile falling over the edges presents a face side about 22 inches (55.9 cm) square. *Note:* By following the directions given here, you can also make a rug or blanket in any size and variation of design you wish. To do so, make a number of flossa sections or strips, in manageable sizes, and join together.

Materials: Sheepswool pelt, 8 by 14 inches (20.3 by 35.6 cm). Sheepswool from Iceland was used because of its 4 to 5 inch (10.2 to 12.7 cm) long hair. Whole pelts or strips are available at some fur stores. Various yarns, ranging from 2- and 3-ply knitting worsted to Icelandic (or Icelandic-type) wool, about 4 ounces: white (3 ounces), and brown and black (1 ounce). Cotton-wrapped polyester thread for machine. Background fabric, 16 by 32 inches (40.6 by 81.3 cm). Purchased pillow or polyester fiberfill stuffing (make a pillow case to contain stuffing, if you wish). Flossa frame, 8 inches (20.3 cm) wide for a 4 inch (10.2 cm) pile. Tape.

Note: For a rug background, use canvas or other closely woven, strong fabric. For a blanket, use a soft fabric. After joining, back the rug with a stiff or rubberized backing; add a lining to the blanket.

Technique: Use short straight stitch or small zigzag for yarn, long zigzag for fur (needle penetrations placed closely together could cause pelt to rip). For instructions on making a flossa frame, refer to the beginning of this section.

Directions: Cut pelts into 3 strips: one, 14 by 2 inches (35.6 by 5.1 cm); two, 14 by 3 inches (35.6 by 7.6 cm). Cut on the skin side with a sharp single-edged razor blade or mat knife, taking care not to cut the wool hairs. Pull the hairs apart to separate them after cutting through the pelt. Cut fabric into two pieces, each 16 inches (40.6 cm) square, for front and back. This includes 1 inch (2.5 cm) seam allowances. On the face fabric, draw or stitch parallel, lengthwise lines, starting and ending 1 inch (2.5 cm) from each edge, and at these intervals: 3, 1, 1, 1, 2, 1, 1, 1, 3 inches (7.6, 2.5, 2.5, 2.5, 5.1, 2.5, 2.5, 2.5, 7.6 cm). (See Figure 5-16.)

To begin, position a 3 inch (7.6 cm) wool strip in the first 3 inch (7.6 cm) section **(Row 1),** side edges on the lines. To keep the wool out of the way while stitching, tape it down ½ inch (1.3 cm) in from each edge. Stitch down both sides of the strip, placing stitches on the pelt. Use a wedge-point needle if necessary. After stitching, remove the tape from the inner edge; the outer edge remains taped until all the rows are completed.

For **Row 2,** wind yarn on the flossa frame, center the frame on the line, and stitch down. The 1 inch (2.5 cm) spaces on each side of this row and other flossa rows are to accommodate the overlapping 4 inch (10.2 cm) flossa pile.

In **Row 3,** introduce the contrast-

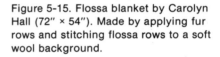

Figure 5-15. Flossa blanket by Carolyn Hall (72″ × 54″). Made by applying fur rows and stitching flossa rows to a soft wool background.

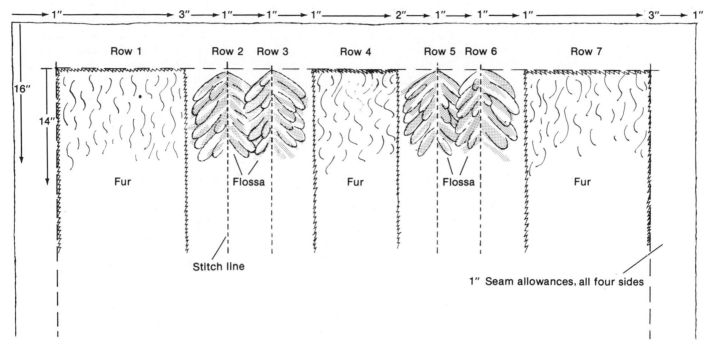

Row 1   Row 2   Row 3   Row 4   Row 5   Row 6   Row 7

16"

14"

Fur   Flossa   Fur   Flossa   Fur

Stitch line

1" Seam allowances, all four sides

Figure 5-16. Pattern for fur and flossa pillow.

Figure 5-17. Fur and flossa Pillow (14" × 14"). You can make a number of flossa sections of any size, and join them to produce a rug or blanket.

ing yarns. After every 1½ inches of (3.8 cm) of white yarn, wind on 1 inch (2.5 cm) of brown and black. Cut the loops in this row. In all other flossa rows, the loops are left uncut.

In **Row 4,** tape the wool strip as before; remove tape from both edges once the strip is stitched down. **Rows 5 and 6** are flossa rows. **Row 7** repeats Row 1, the tape on the outer edge remains in place. You can do the wool rows first, if you prefer. (*Note:* If you are making a rug or a blanket, the following instructions do not apply.) When you have completed all the rows, pin front and back together, right sides facing. Brush the yarn and wool away from the seam lines first so that they will not be stitched in. Tape them down if you wish. Because you want to see the existing stitch lines, work with the front side facing up. Stitch all around, leaving a 6 inch (15.2 cm) opening for turning and stuffing. Stitch the pelt edges into these seams by stitching over the existing stitch lines. Trim seams and turn cover rightside out. Remove all tape very carefully. Stuff the cover and hand-stitch the seam shut.

65

ART PROTIS TAPESTRY

Invented in Czechoslovakia, the "Art Protis" machine uses zigzag stitches to stitch layers of yarn, fabrics, and loose fibers into a tapestry in a considerably shorter length of time than it would take by more traditional methods. The fibers are laid onto a backing fabric and are compressed with a sheet of heavy plastic. Fibers and backing, minus the plastic, are fed through the ma-chine, which has hundreds of nee-dles, spaced about ¼ inch (.6 cm) apart, each with its own thread sup-ply. The result is a soft- or hard-edged design, muted or bold, in a great or limited variety of colors and textures.

This innovative method of ma-chine couching can be simulated on your own sewing machine.

You will need a firm fabric for the backing. Gather together an assort-ment of thin or heavy yarns, unspun fibers, and pieces of fabric. Lay these on the backing to build up your de-sign. Move the materials about, reposition some here, some there, until you are satisfied with the com-position. Then compress the result with a heavy sheet of clear plastic or with a pane of glass to see how the piece will look when completed. If you still approve of the design, baste or pin the materials in place, or sandwich the piece between the plas-tic sheet and a cardboard backing taped together along one side.

If the piece is large, give yourself plenty of room in which to sew it. Arrange the sewing machine so it is away from the wall and on or next to a large table. The surface of the table should be level with the sewing machine bed. An alternate method might be to work in sections which are then joined together to make a larger piece.

Set the machine for zigzag stitch at its widest. Use the zigzag presser foot and tape a double thickness of

Figure 5-18. Art Protis tapestry by Robert Freimark. Unspun wool fibers stitched with a multi-needle machine.

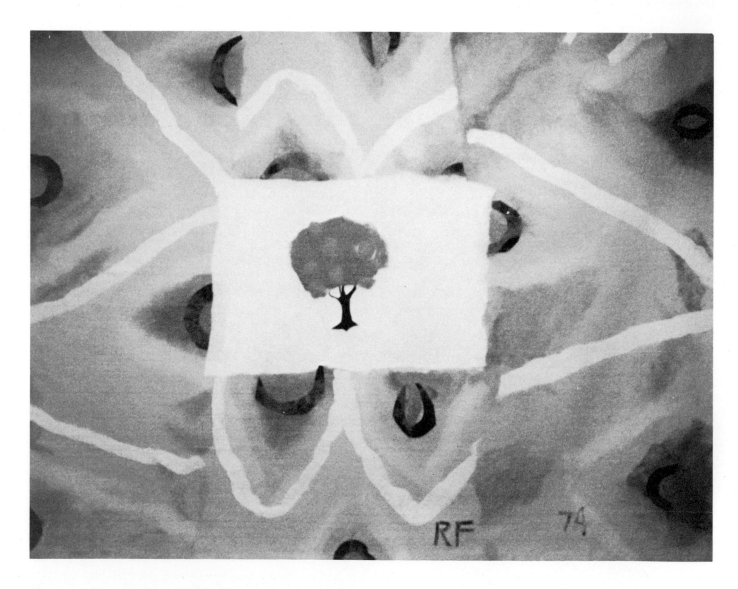

masking tape across its toes at the front to prevent their tangling in the yarns (see Figure 5-12).

If you pinned or basted the piece, stitch around its edges first, then spiral inward. If you are using the plastic/cardboard panel, slide the panel back just enough to expose one end for stitching; continue to expose more as you stitch across the rows. Stitch the entire design, or just those areas you want stitched down; the movement of the stitches can also become part of the design. Use your fingers or a pair of long tweezers to guide the fibers under the presser foot.

Once this stitching is completed, add other yarns and/or fabrics if you wish. Layer certain areas to make some higher, some lower; introduce . additional color; try out various objects to enhance the design. One thing will lead to another, and you

will find yourself thinking of all sorts of ingenious ways to construct novel Art Protis pieces. This technique offers a wide latitude for creative expression in form, design, and color.

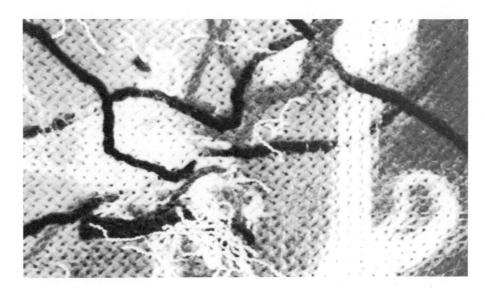

Figure 5-19. (Detail) *Modulation in All Things* by Robert Freimark (11' × 14'8"). Tapestry.

Figure 5-21. *Calligraphy* by Carolyn Hall (18" × 24"). Simulated Art Protis tapestry.

Figure 5-20. Detail of yarns and unspun fibers zigzag-stitched onto background fabric to simulate the Art Protis technique. Note tape across presser foot toes to prevent yarns and fibers catching in the slot.

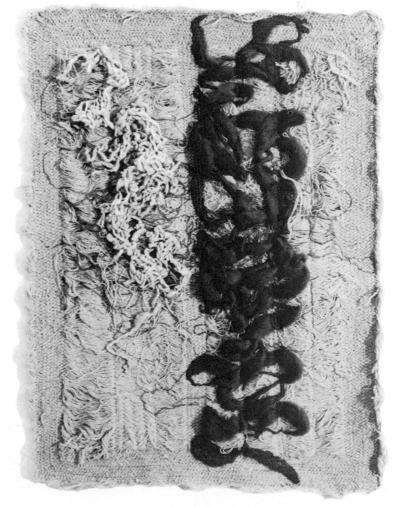

6. BASKETRY

Practically anything can be made on a sewing machine: clothing, bedding, tents, boats, kites, sails, toys, art .... But what about baskets? Never having seen a machine-sewn basket, I decided to make one using the coiling technique, and found the technique very adaptable to the machine. Not only baskets, but mats, totes, hats, and rugs can be made by this method as well. The material, depending on the project, can be yarn, felt strips, or any cord or rope that will fit under the presser foot (without raising it too high) and that can be easily pierced with a needle.

Set the machine for wide zigzag or blind hem stitch. Use a zigzag presser foot. Thread the machine with a strong thread, such as cotton-wrapped polyester, in a color to contrast with or match the cord (or other material) to be coiled.

Starting A Basket. To make the starting coil, taper the end of the cord to reduce bulk, then bend the cord so it turns and meets itself (Figure 6-1, *A*). Using the diagram as a guide, begin stitching at the top of the join. If this area is too thick for the needle to pierce, begin just below it. While stitching, hold the join tightly so that the stitches catch on both sides, pulling the sides close together.

Coil the cord around the join and stitch together (Figure 6-1, *B*). Keeping the coils flat, continue coiling and stitching until you have made a base in the size you want.

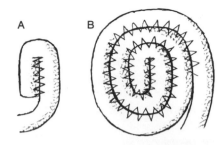

Figure 6-1. To start basket: (*a*) Beginning join. (*b*) Stitch coils together.

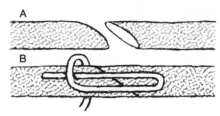

Figure 6-2. To join ends: (*a*) Cut at an angle. (*b*) Wrap to cover join.

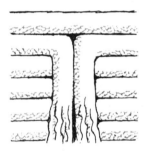

Figure 6-3. For a variation, fray the ends then join the cords. They will be secured when stitched to next round.

Forming The Sides. To form rounded sides, hold the base at a slightly sharper angle than you want the finished sides to assume. Start the next coil over the previous coil so that an outward slant will be established. Shape the sides as you go by adjusting the slant (see Figure 6-5). To form straight sides, place coils directly over each other.

Introducing Color. You can introduce color by wrapping the cord with yarn or embroidery thread. To wrap,

Figure 6-4. Machine sewn basket and mat by Carolyn Hall. Nylon parachute cord. Note frayed and knotted ends set off with beads.

lay an end of the yarn or thread about 2 or 3 inches (5 or 7 cm) along the cord, turn it at right angles to itself (see Figure 6-2, B), hold firmly, and begin wrapping. The first and succeeding rounds will cover the end. Wrap firmly, taking care that each round lies neatly against the one before. Coil and stitch the wrapped section to the previous coil.

If wrapping will be extensive, or if you want to change color, wrap until only a few inches of yarn or thread remain, then lay the tail end along the cord and the new end alongside. Hold both tightly and resume wrapping. The ends will be covered by succeeding rounds.

How To Treat Cord Ends. To end one cord and begin another, wrap the old and new ends firmly with string or thread to prevent fraying; hold one end against the other and continue stitching. The next round will secure the ends in place. For a neater joining, taper the ends or cut them at an angle so they overlap when fitted together, then wrap the join with yarn or thread. Hold the join tightly and continue stitching. You can also macrame, knot, or fray the ends. Note the frayed ends in Figure 6-3; the old end was allowed to hang loosely, and the new end was placed parallel to it. Both were joined as shown in the diagram. The ends can be frayed, or treated in other ways, before or after the basket is completed. Beads can also be slipped onto the ends (see Figure 6-4). To vary the coiling pattern further, loop the cord occasionally and stitch it in place; a series of loops can form open areas (see Figure 6-7). Also, while stitching a basket, you can sculpture it to interesting shapes.

Figure 6-5. To shape a rounded form, hold at an angle while stitching coils.

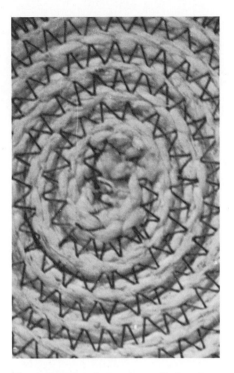

Figure 6-6. Detail showing coiled and stitched base.

Figure 6-7. Freeform basket by Carolyn Hall. Cotton clothesline, wrapped occasionally with yarn. For color, see C-6.

7. PATCHWORK

Patchwork, the piecing together of small pieces of fabric to make a larger piece of fabric, is an American folk art. The first women settlers, piecing their treasured fabric patches together to make quilts, developed a style and a technique, and established a tradition. Out of their domestic thrift and inborn sense of design came quilts of originality and real beauty. Some of these quilts can be seen in museums today.

Although quilts have always been an important part of patchwork, the fabric patches are equally useful for making clothing, bags, pillows, curtains, wall hangings, and more. Any fabric, from denim to flannel to velvet, purchased new or at rummage sales, or remnants on hand can be used. Bold plaids, delicate prints, nostalgic calicoes, bright or muted solids can all be combined in the same piece, as long as they are compatible in color, texture, character, and method of cleaning. Choose your colors and plan the color repeats wisely, for these are the links that unify the patchwork piece into a harmonious whole.

TECHNIQUE

When planning a patchwork project, first decide on the overall size, then on the size of a single shape. The easiest shapes are the traditional straight-line geometrics—diamonds, triangles, squares, hexagons. Make a template by drawing the shape with

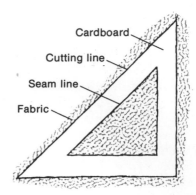

Figure 7-1. Window template enables you to mark cutting line and seam line at the same time.

ruler and pencil onto something sturdy, such as a manila folder or a piece of cardboard. Include seam allowances of ¼ to ½ inch (.6 to 1.3 cm) or more, depending on the fabrics. Cut the template out.

Place the template on the wrong side of the fabric, trace its outlines, and cut the shape out. Draw the sewing lines on the fabric.

Figure 7-2. Design variations.

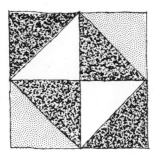  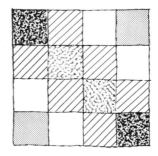 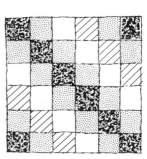

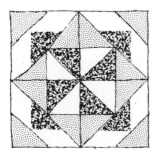 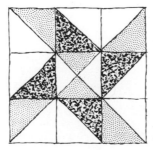 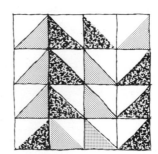 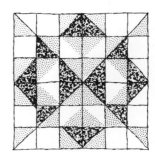

Be careful not to stretch the fabric while tracing or cutting. Precision in cutting is very important; all sides must be exactly even for the finished patchwork to lie smoothly and evenly. Replace templates if their edges are worn from marking. You could also make a window template, that is, a template with its center cut out so that the sewing line and seam line can be marked at the same time (see Figure 7-1). Draw the shape onto cardboard, as before, and mark seam allowances all around. Then score and cut along the inner and outer lines. A window template may not be necessary for squares but may be helpful for other shapes.

Next, decide on the arrangement of the shapes, moving them about until you are satisfied with the result. For a large design, it will be easier if you pin the patches to brown wrapping paper, the same size as the project, then unpin them as you rearrange the pattern. Once the patches are arranged to your liking, be sure to draw a diagram to help you remember placement. Now you are ready to begin sewing them together.

Assembling the Patches. Hold or pin two patches together, right sides facing, lengthwise edges matching. Straight-stitch along the sewing line, following it exactly. Tie off each pair separately or stitch several units together, kite-tail fashion, leaving enough thread between each pair for tying off. Press seams before cutting joined patches apart. Join horizontal rows, pinning first to match all seams exactly, then sew together with a long seam. With your fingers, press seams to one side as you sew, preferably toward the darker fabric. With heavy fabric, press seams open. Squares can also be joined horizontally and vertically in blocks; join from the center out to ensure smoothness. Trim excess seam allowances diagonally at the intersections to avoid fabric bunching. As you work, measure the blocks to check accuracy.

Figure 7-3. Star pattern.

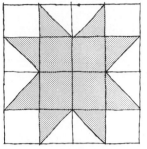
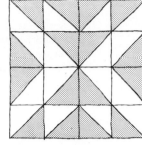
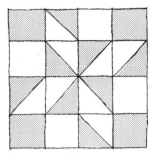

Variation 1:2 colors   Variation 2:2 colors   Variation 3:2 colors

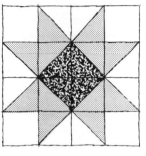
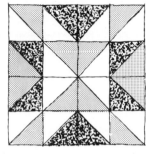
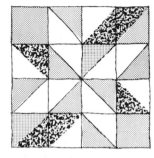

Variation 1:3 colors   Variation 2:3 colors   Variation 3:3 colors

Figure 7-4. Patchwork pillow (16″ × 16″). Some triangles are outlined with satin stitch to form a design within a design.

71

Patchwork Tote or Pillow: Project

Finished Size: Approximately 16 by 16 inches (40 by 40 cm).

Materials: Velveteen and corduroy in various colors for front, about ½ yard (46cm) of 36-inch (91cm) fabric (see *Note* below) ; velveteen or corduroy, 17½ by 17½ inches (44.5 by 44.5 cm) for back—¾ inch (1.8cm) seam allowances included. *Tote:* flannel, 2 pieces, each 17½ by 17½ inches (44.5 by 44.5cm), for lining; velveteen strip, 24 by 4 inches (61 by 10.2cm), for shoulder strap; 15 inch (38.1cm) plastic zipper. *Pillow:* purchased pillow or polyester fiberfill stuffing.

Note: 32 triangles, 5½ by 5½ by 7½ inches (14 by 14 by 19.1cm) each, for pillow or tote are cut from the face fabric. Seam allowances of ¾ inch (1.8cm) are included. Triangles are arranged into 16 squares, 4 rows of 4 squares each.

Directions: Make a triangular template, 5½ by 5½ by 7½ inches (14 by 14 by 19.1cm). Or, make two templates by drawing a 5½ inch (14cm) square and cutting it in half diagonally.

Lay face fabric wrong side up. Place the template with its shorter sides along the grain and its diagonal on the bias. Trace around the template, draw the sewing lines on the fabric, and cut out the patches. Make 32 triangles.

When all the triangles are cut, begin arranging them into squares. Since there are 32 triangles to be arranged into 16 squares, you will have a number of design and color options. You may even want to cut additional triangles and then assemble combinations until you find a design that "sings" to you. Once you have settled on a design, write the color order on a diagram as a handy reference.

With right sides facing, pin tri-

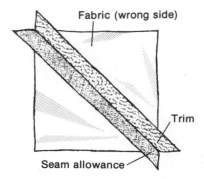

Figure 7-6. Trim excess allowances diagonally.

angles together along the bias edges and begin sewing them into squares. If necessary, ease presser foot pressure to prevent fabrics from sliding on each other. Sew exactly on the sewing lines. Measure squares to check accuracy. If any squares are not true to size, remove stitches and start again, or compensate on other seams by taking larger or smaller allowances. Press seams open with your fingers as you sew. Trim excess seam allowance at corners (Figure 7-6).

To assemble, join together the four squares that will form the center of the design. Join the remaining squares in horizontal and vertical rows. Make sure that all seams meet exactly at the intersections. Press seams open and trim excess.

The completed front can now be machine embroidered from the face or reverse side, if you wish. Run designs at random for a "crazy quilt" effect (see Figure 7-7).

Pillow. To assemble the pillow, pin front and back together, right sides facing. Cut to fit if necessary. Stitch around, leaving an opening on one side for pillow or stuffing. Trim seams and corners, and turn rightside out. Stuff firmly or insert pillow. Stitch seam closed.

Tote. You can leave the back fabric unadorned, embroider it with a

Figure 7-5. Patchwork tote (16″ × 16″). Note that triangles are arranged differently than those in Figure 7-4.

free motion design, or patch it to resemble the front.

Refer to Figure 7-8 while assembling. Lay front fabric face up. Place zipper face down, its outside edge along the top edge of the fabric, and stitch in place. Lay one lining piece over and stitch it down along the same seam line. Sew the other edge of the zipper and the other lining to the back in the same manner.

Open the zipper and lay the fabric flat, lining to lining and back to front. Stitch around, starting at one corner of the lining and ending at the opposite corner so that the lining remains open at the bottom.

Make the shoulder strap next. Fold the velveteen strip in half lengthwise, right sides facing. Stitch a ½ inch (1.3cm) seam along the lengthwise raw edges. Turn the strip rightside out. Topstitch both lengthwise edges. Stitch each end of the strip to each end of the zipper fabric by hand or machine. Reinforce the stitching. A plastic zipper is wide enough to accommodate the width

of the strip, but measure first to be sure, and taper the ends of the strip, if necessary.

To finish assembling the tote, trim seams and turn rightside out. Fold under the opening in the lining and stitch shut. Tuck the lining into the tote.

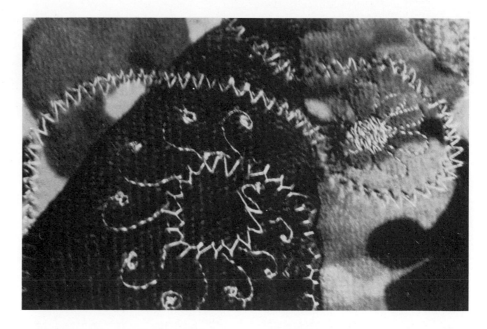

Figure 7-7. Detail of patchwork tote. Free motion straight and zigzag stitches decorate surface in a "crazy quilt" manner.

Figure 7-8. Assembling tote.

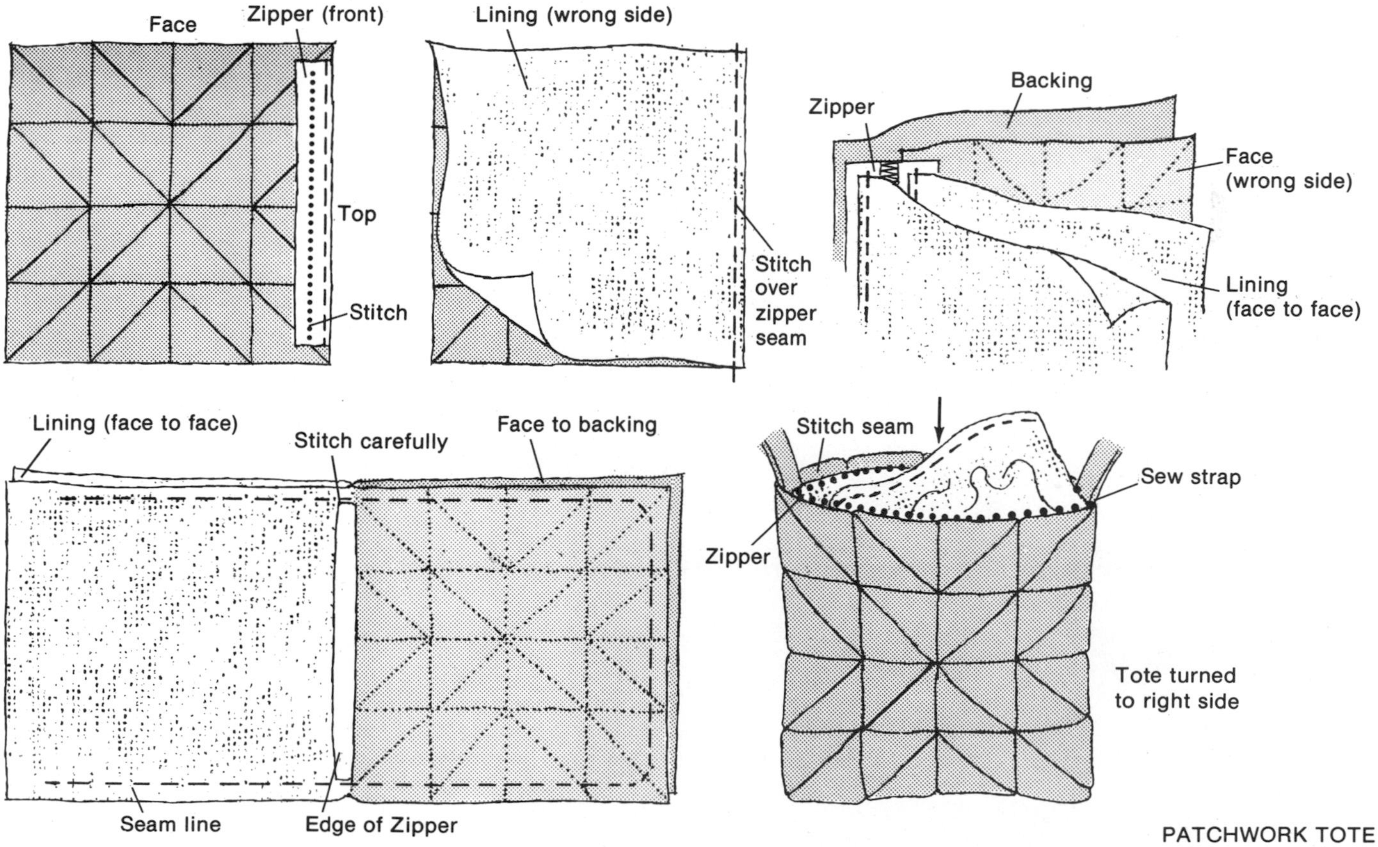

PATCHWORK TOTE

73

Flag: Project

Finished Size: 39 by 62 inches (99.1 by 157.5cm).

Materials: Lightweight fabrics (cotton, rayon, silk, wool, lace, etc.), about 1 yard (91.4cm) each in red (solids, prints, woven designs), white (variety of textures), blue (solids, prints). Fabric for back, 40 by 63 inches (101.6 by 160cm). Ribbon, 40 by 3 inches (101.6 by 7.6cm).

Note: All pieces are joined with ½ inch (1.3cm) seams; seam allowances are included in the dimensions. Press seams to the darker side after sewing.

Directions: Cut the reds, and most of the whites, into patches, 2 to 6 inches (5.1 to 15.2cm) long by 4 inches (10.2cm) wide (the remaining white fabric will be cut later to form stars). Depending on the fabric, an easy way to get uniform widths is to mark the top of the fabric at 4 inch

(10.2cm) intervals, clip the marks, and tear fabric into strips with swift, downward motions in the direction of the grain. Lay one strip on another, mark at 2 to 6 inch (5.1 to 15.2cm) intervals, and cut.

Pin the reds together, end to end, to make 3 stripes, each 61 by 4 inches (154.9 by 10.2cm), and 4 stripes, each 34 by 4 inches (86.4 by 10.2cm). Press seams to one side with your fingers as you pin. The overall effect will be enhanced if patches of different lengths alternate.

Pin whites in the same manner and make 3 stripes, each 61 by 4 inches (154.9 by 10.2cm), and 3 stripes, each 34 by 4 inches (86.4 by 10.2cm).

Cut the blues into 63 patches, each 4 inches (10.2cm) square. Alternate solids and prints, and stitch together to make 7 strips of 9 squares each. Then stitch the strips to form a checkered pattern (see Figure 7-9). The blue field of 63 3-inch (7.6cm) squares, plus ½ inch (1.3cm) seams on the outside, will be 22 by 28 inches (55.9 by 71.1cm).

Make a template for the stars (see Figure 7-10 for a full-size pattern).

Figure 7-10. Pattern for 2½-inch (6.4cm) star. Add ¼-inch seam allowance if hemming.

Cut 13 stars out of white fabric. Space them evenly to form a circle on the blue field. Hem the stars, or else attach them to the fabric with straight stitch and cover the raw edges with a narrow satin stitch.

Join the 34-inch (86.4cm) red and white stripes, stitching each to the next, face to face. Alternate the colors, starting and ending with red. After joining, stitch the section to the blue field, matching seams exactly. Trim corners.

Join the 61-inch (154.9cm) stripes, starting with white and ending with red. Then, join the two halves of the flag together. Sew the ribbon along the blue-field side of the flag; allow ½ inch (1.3cm) seams for a finished width of 2 inches (5.1 cm). Press the flag. Lay the backing on, face to face, and stitch all around, leaving a 6-inch (15.2cm) opening for turning. Trim corners at an angle. Turn rightside out, stitch the opening closed, and press the flag again.

Figure 7-9. *American Symbols* by Carolyn Hall (39" × 62"). For color, see C-8.

SEMINOLE INDIAN PATCHWORK

The Seminole Indians of Florida are noted for their handsome geometric patchwork designs. These colorful patterns, developed just after the first hand-cranked sewing machines were introduced, look extremely complex but are actually relatively simple to design and sew. Fabrics of two or more colors are cut or torn into strips and seamed horizontally to form striped bands The bands are then cut vertically or diagonally and restitched to form a design. Many intricate-looking patterns can be created by cutting the bands further and restitching.

For example, to make a 16 by 16 inch (40.6 by 40.6cm) checkered pattern, cut or tear a dark-colored fabric into 4 strips, each 24 inches (61cm) long by 3 inches (7.6cm) wide—½ inch (1.3cm) seam allowances included. Cut 4 identical strips from light-colored fabric. Alternate light and dark strips and stitch together, side by side, to make a striped fabric, 17 by 24 inches (43.2 by 61cm). Press seams to one side. Then cut across the strips every 3 inches (7.6cm) to make 8 strips of alternating squares. Reverse every other strip, and stitch together to form a checkered pattern, 17 by 17 inches (43.2 by 43.2cm) with ½ inch (1.3cm) seams on the outside. For a zigzag pattern, make two identical striped bands. Cut one band diagonally into strips. From the other band, cut an equal number of strips diagonally in the opposite direction. Stitch together, alternating the slant of the stripes to form a zigzag. Work all patterns out on graph paper before cutting the fabric.

For another variation, sew strips of different widths together. This could be carefully planned, as in the

Figure 7-11. Seminole purse. Rows of rickrack braid form borders at top and bottom. (Courtesy, Donald J. and Marsha A. Mettler)

Figure 7-12. Detail of Seminole-style skirt by Donald J. and Marsha A. Mettler shows a variety of design arrangements.

Seminole work, or assembled at random, letting the stripes meet by chance.

Other ways to vary or embellish this technique will occur to you as you work. In recent years, rickrack braid has been substituted for the narrow, solid color rows that were once used to set off border patterns. This substitution offends traditionalists, but change is the one constant you can depend on. You could use a variety of fabric combinations (including prints and an occasional transparent material), machine-embroider the pieces, topstitch or stuff them, make the fabric into clothing, rugs, or wall hangings, and more.

Figure 7-13. Making a Seminole purse.

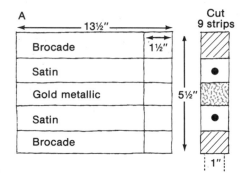

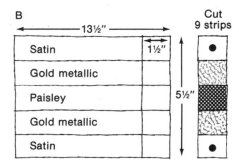

Purse, Seminole Style: Project

Finished Size: 12 by 12 inches (30.5 by 30.5cm).

Materials: Silver metallic, gold metallic, gold satin, white and gold brocade, red and gold paisley (see note below for amounts). Quilted lining, 24½ by 12 inches (62.2 by 30.5 cm). Ties, two lengths of macrame cord, each 24 inches (61cm).

Note: Cut fabric to these dimensions:
Silver metallic:
    2 strips, 24½ by 4½ inches (62.2 by 11.4cm)
    6 strips, 5½ by 1½ inches (14 by 3.8cm)
Gold metallic:
    3 strips, 13½ by 1½ inches (34.3 by 3.8cm)
Brocade:
    2 strips, 13½ by 1½ inches (34.3 by 3.8cm)
Satin:
    4 strips, 13½ by 1½ inches (34.3 by 3.8cm)
Paisley:
    1 strip, 13½ by 1½ inches (34.3 by 3.8cm)

Join all pieces with ¼ inch (.6cm) seams. Press seams to one side after sewing. Follow diagrams throughout.

Pattern for Completed Band

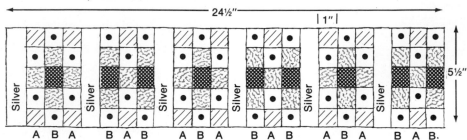

Directions: *To form bands:* For band *A,* join strips along their lengths in the following order, as shown in Figure 7-13: brocade, satin, gold metallic, satin, brocade. For band *B,* join strips in the same manner, and in the following order: satin, gold metallic, paisley, gold metallic, satin. Each band will be approximately 5½ by 13½ inches (14 by 34.3cm). Cut *A* every 1½ inches (3.8cm) to make 9 strips, each 5½ by 1½ inches (14 by 3.8cm). Repeat for *B.*

Restitch strips to make 6 bands of 3 strips each. Join the bands, alternating them with the 5½ by 1½ inch (14 by 3.8cm) silver strips. Completed band will be approximately 5½ by 24½ inches (14 by 62.2 cm). *Note:* Each square may be less than 1 by 1 inch (2.5 by 2.5cm). Stitch one 24½ by 4½ inch (62.2 by 11.4cm) silver strip to the top of the band, and the other silver strip to the bottom of the band, long sides matching. Pin quilted lining over, face to face. Sew across the top to join. Where indicated on the diagram, make a regular or bound buttonhole for insertion of ties. Lay lining to lining and back to front. Stitch as shown. Leave another opening for ties on the seam line, and reinforce stitching at that point. Leave an opening for turning. Trim seams, turn right side out, and sew opening shut. Tuck lining into the purse. Stitch ¾ inch (1.8cm) from the top seam to make a carrier for the ties. Insert ties and pull through, using a safety pin as an aid.

Figure 7-14. Purse, Seminole style (12″ × 12″).

Figure 7-15. Assembling purse.

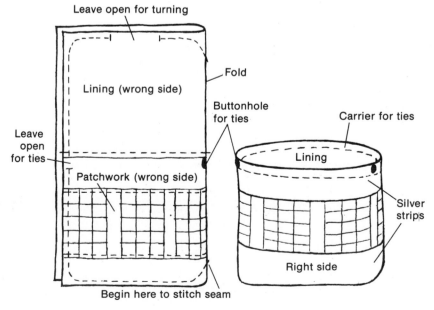

8. APPLIQUÉ

Appliqué is an appealing and versatile way to achieve color, texture, and variety of line. In this technique, shaped pieces of fabric are laid onto a background fabric and are stitched to it. The stitching can be purely functional, the stitches visible or invisible, so that emphasis is on the contrasting shapes; or it can be decorative and serve to supplement the character of the shaped pieces. The very nature of appliqué lends itself to a number of variations. Appliqué can also be successfully combined with patchwork and quilting.

In addition to a vast assortment of plain and printed fabrics and a variety of stitches, threads can be used to further enhance the piece. Heavy threads provide additional texture; elegant silk or other shiny

threads, a rich glow. Two threads combined in the same needle provide a colorful counterpoint.

TECHNIQUE

First decide on the texture, color, and size of the background fabric, then select the materials for the design shapes. If the piece will be washed, use colorfast fabrics and preshrink them. Determine the elements of your design by making a sketch or by cutting shapes out of paper and moving them about on the background. For multiples of the same motif, make a cardboard template for each design shape.

Appliqué does not have the limitations of fitted patchwork pieces. Its lines are completely free and can be cut to any shape: forms found in nature, pictorial figures, geometric abstractions, or graphic designs. Patterns can be as simple or as intricate as you wish. Pieces can overlap or be laid onto one another. Because the background can be so quickly covered, you can plan large-scale projects such as wall hangings, banners, or quilts. Or you may consider the appliqué as a background for elaborate stitchery, or as a collage enriched with a tracery of delicate embroidery.

There are two methods of dealing with appliqué shapes. Depending on the fabric, the stitches to be used, and the design requirements, you can either hem the shapes first and then stitch them down, or stitch them down first and then trim raw edges or leave them exposed.

Mark the design on the background fabric and cut the design shapes. On shapes that will be hemmed, notch any curved edges so that, when turned back, the contours will be smooth. For a smoother curve, run a line of basting stitches, pull one thread to gather, and press. If there are small folds in the gathered hem that will not press flat, notch the edges. Another way is to turn the edges over cardboard that is cut to the shape and press edges flat. On

shapes that will be trimmed after being stitched down, mark the stitch line all around. Pin or baste the shapes securely in place on the background fabric. Use slender pins to avoid distorting the fabric.

Any stitch can be used in appliqué. A line of *straight stitch* is the simplest and quickest of all. Since this stitch has no width to speak of, and therefore cannot cover an edge, it is best to turn hems under for a crisp, neat finish. Or use fabrics with selvages (woven edges), such as ribbons, or those with nonfraying edges, such as felt or suede. Shapes can be secured first with straight stitch or narrow zigzag, and then outlined with a more decorative stitch or a couched line of yarn.

The *zigzag stitch* moves back and forth over an edge without covering it completely. If shapes are unhemmed, this stitch will not cover the raw edges, but, with proper handling, these casually stitched-down edges can have a free, random, painterly effect, with emphasis more on design then technique. *Satin stitch* completely covers an edge and is the most popular way to outline a shape. A wide width satin stitch in a contrasting color becomes a strong element in the design. This stitch is usually used to cover the preliminary straight or narrow zigzag stitch that holds the shape in place.

The *blind hem stitch* tacks a turned hem much in the same inconspicuous way as does the whip stitch in hand sewing. Since the hem is caught only at intervals, a rhythmic series of indentations results (see Figure 8-13).

Some machines have an *automatic pattern stitch* that resembles the handsewn buttonhole stitch. An open stitch such as this looks best on a firm-edged or hemmed shape. If the pattern stitch is wide enough to cover a preliminary row of stitches (straight stitch or narrow zigzag), it will not be necessary to hem the piece.

If the shapes shift on the background fabric while being stitched,

pin-baste them securely, or adhere with either fabric glue or a bonding fabric. Or tape them down and peel off the tape as you come to it. If the fabric puckers, use a hoop or back the background fabric with paper. If the shape is large, use newspaper. When one shape overlaps another, leave the raw edges flat wherever they will be covered.

Figure 8-2. Jester puppet by Carolyn Hall. Straight stitch applique. Edges of printed fabric exposed in some areas, hemmed in others. Non-fraying felt and suede stitched along raw edges.

Leave thread ends long enough at the beginning and end of all stitching to be pulled through to the back and tied. When stitching is completed, remove any basting threads not covered by the outline stitches. Cut away excess from the untrimmed shapes. Use small, sharp scissors, and cut close to the outline, holding scissors so that the left blade is against the stitch line (see Figure 8-21). It may help to fold excess over your finger so that the edge will be more exposed. If it is any comfort, nearly everyone cuts into the background fabric on the first try.

ALPHABETS FOR APPLIQUÉ

Letters or numbers can be incorporated in a design, can form the basis of a design, or can become the subject of an entire piece. To add a personal imprint to your work, make a monogram.

Figure 8-3. *Golden Five* by Robert Indiana. Appliquéd felt banner. (Courtesy, Multiples, Inc. New York, New York)

Figure 8-4. *Campbell's Soup* by Andy Warhol (90½" × 56¼"). Felt banner. 1966. (Collection, The Museum of Modern Art, New York. Gift of Philip Johnson)

Figure 8-5. Two suggested alphabets for appliqué.

C-1. **(Left)** *Sugar Top* by Verina Warren. Wall hanging. Machine embroidery combined with hand stitching.

C-2. **(Lower left)** Detail, *Gold Thistle* by Edith Pirtle. Appliqué and free motion embroidery on velvet. Decoration on garment. (Courtesy, Cynthia Walgren)

C-3. **(Right)** *Triton* by Janet Kuemmerlein. Wall hanging. A stitched and stuffed fiber sculpture. (Courtesy, Northfield Hilton Hotel)

C-4. **(Left)** *Polish Rider (Homage to Rembrandt)* by Robert Freimark (6'4" × 8'6"). Tapestry in the Art Protis technique.

C-5. **(Right)** *Gothic Window* by Robert Freimark. Closeup of the Art Protis technique. Note that zigzag stitches cover entire surface of unspun fibers and yarns.

C-6. **(Lower right)** Machine-sewn basket by Carolyn Hall. Clothesline wrapped with yarn in areas.

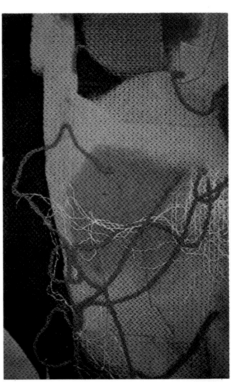

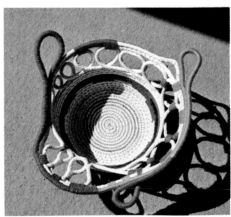

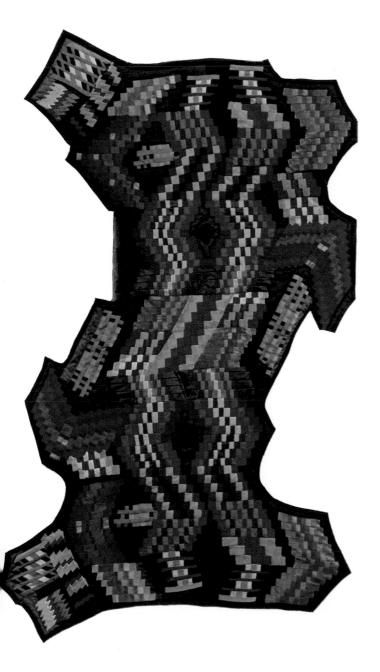

C-7. **(Left)** Wall hanging by Helen Bitar (79″ × 46″). Seminole-style patchwork technique.

C-8. **(Right)** *American Symbols* by Carolyn Hall (3′ × 5′). Patchwork.

C-9. **(Lower right)** *Hill School* by Carolyn Hall. Panel from bicentennial banner.

C-10. **(Left)** *Still Life* by Margaret Cusack (17″ × 15″). Appliqued collage hanging created for a magazine illustration.

C-11. **(Right)** Detail of banner by Norman LaLiberté. Appliquéd with satin stitch.

C-12. **(Lower Right).** *Fish Hanging* by Sara Cibelli (30″ × 24″). Appliquéd cotton with polyester batting.

C-13. **(Left)** *Celestial Landscape* by Lenore Davis (44½" × 34" × ¼"). Wall hanging. Quilted and dyed cotton velveteen.

C-14. **(Right)** *Atlanta Skyline* by Karen E. Reese (6' × 5½' × 2"). A fabric painting. Cotton and organza, stuffed and dyed. Photograph by Samuel B. Frank. (Courtesy, Carter and Assoc., Atlanta, Georgia)

C-15. **(Lower right)** Detail, *Wildflower Quilt* by Sara Drower (48" sq.). Painted in permanent dyes on cotton polyester.

C-16 & C-17. **(Left)** *A. Pancakes Cookbook: Eat It!* by Alice Whitman Leeds (9′ in diameter; opens to 9″ × 80″; plate, 13″). Stack of eight suede pancakes on a satin plate. **(Right)** Note machine-stitched recipes and drawings. Quilted and dyed.

C-18. **(Lower left)** *Gourds* by Nancy McAfee (each approximately 10″ × 8″). Batik-dyed cotton fabric, stitched and stuffed.

C-19. **(Lower right)** *Babar and Celeste* by Dee Durkee (each 9″ × 4″ × 2″). Soft sculpture figures. Stitched and stuffed canvas, painted with acrylics and ink.

C-20. **(Left)** *Macaw* by Carolyn Hall (24″ tall). A realistic stuffed shape.

C-21. **(Right)** *Radish* by Betsy Meyers (3′ × 6′). Bean bag chair. Machine-sewn on corduroy, flannel, and upholstery velvet. (Courtesy, Robert Meyers)

C-22. **(Lower left)** *U.S. Puzzle* by Carolyn Hall (36″ × 60″ × 4″).

C-23. **(Lower right)** *Tribute to Michigan Weather* by Douglas Alden Peterson (8′ × 9′ × 6″). Window piece. Photograph by Dick Havens. (Courtesy, Audrey Designs)

C-24. **(Left)** *Medallion* by Carolyn Hall
(81″ × 21″). Stuffed hanging.

C-25. **(Right)** *Garibaldi* by Karen Elizabeth
Reese (8′ × 5′ × 1′). Soft sculpture portrait.
Stitched, stuffed, and embroidered pillow
forms assembled to create wall hanging.
Photograph by Donald Campbell.
(Courtesy, Tony Smith)

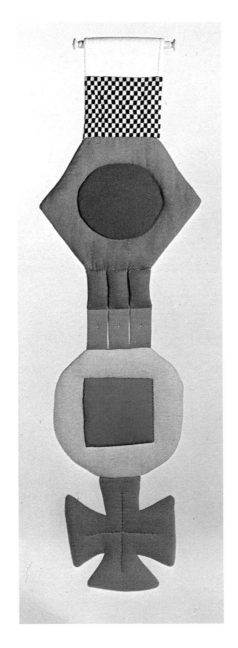

Name Pillows: Project

Materials: Assorted fabrics in related colors for appliqué shapes. Fabric for front and back; cut to your pillow size and allow for seams. If a zipper will be inserted, add an extra 2 inch (5.1cm) allowance on the back. Purchase a pillow or make your own with cotton fabric for the case and polyester fiberfill for the stuffing.

Directions: Design a name for the pillow. To help with design ideas, think of the person who will be receiving the pillow. For example, plaid was chosen for "S.G." (Figure 8-7) because of his Scottish ancestry.

Large, simply shaped letters work best for appliqué. Sketch the name or initials in various type faces and see what develops. Try squeezing, elongating, or overlapping the letters. Suggested lettering styles for appliqué are shown in Figure 8-5. Also study advertisements in magazines and newspapers, and note the imaginative ways graphic artists use letters.

The designs can be worked out on paper, using a ruler where necessary for guide lines and letters and drawing the remainder free-hand for a relaxed flow. Cut the patterns for the letters. Pin the face fabric to the pillow and lay out the design shapes, arranging them on the flat of the pillow so that no part of a shape is too near a pillow edge. Once the design is pinned in place, remove the face fabric from the pillow and stitch the design according to the technique you have chosen.

Begin assembling the pillow cover. Pin front and back fabrics together, right sides facing. Stitch together, making rounded corners and leaving an opening on one side for the pillow. If you want to insert a zipper, do so before stitching the sides together. The zipper can be on one side or down the center of the back. If the latter, make the appropriate cut in the fabric for insertion. A concealed zipper will look best.

Trim seams to within ¼ inch (.6cm) of the edges. Trim corners and turn the cover rightside out. Insert the pillow. If a zipper is not used, turn the edges of the opening under and stitch closed.

Figure 8-6. Name pillow (17″ × 24″). Letters appliquéd with zigzag stitches, then outlined with satin stitch. Suede cloth, velvet, wool, corduroy. (Courtesy, Dave Goodrich)

Figure 8-7. Name pillow (17″ × 24″). Letters appliquéd with zigzag stitches, plaid squares outlined with couched yarn. Suede cloth and wool. (Courtesy, Steve Goodrich)

ACCESSORY MATERIALS
AND OBJECTS

A variety of materials and objects can be appliquéd to accompany, enhance, or become part of your design—a row of lace, or fur, or a fringe for example. If you stitch nonwoven materials such as Mylar, plastic, paper, or photographs, use long stitches; too many needle holes spaced too close together could cause the materials to tear.

If you are using fabrics or objects that cannot be sewn down, cover them with transparent material, such as nylon stockings or plastic, and stitch the material in place. A fascinating way to create contrasts between silhouetted shapes and fabric is to use sheer fabric for the background. This treatment is illustrated in the project that follows.

Figure 8-8. *Galaxy,* appliquéd hanging by Selma D.J. Hollander (36″ × 34″). A variety of colors, textures, and forms arranged then appliquéd to create a rhythmic design.

Figure 8-9. Detail *Rebirth* by Eleanor R. Bostwick (9′7″ × 3′¼″). Baptismal wall hanging. Appliquéd tafetta and lustrous fabrics. Free motion embroidery in areas.

Sea Shell Curtain: Project

Materials: Purchase a curtain or make your own; the fabric should be translucent, strong, and of good quality. Overlay fabrics: metallic, clear plastic, lace, net, or other sheers. Yarn and metallic threads. A collection of sea shells, starfish, sea horses, and sand dollars.

Note: Plan to hang the curtain so it is either stretched taut between curtain rods at top and bottom, or hanging loosely, but with a limited amount of gathers (too many will obscure the design). If you are making your own curtain, complete it before appliquéing the design.

Directions: Lay the curtain on the floor, or over a sheet on the floor, and secure with masking tape. Cut long freeform shapes from the overlay fabrics, contouring them to simulate the flowing motion of the sea. Arrange on the curtain for the desired effect. Place yarn and metallic thread where you plan to couch them. Position shells and other sea objects to look as if waves left them behind on the sand.

Pin overlays, yarn, and thread to the curtain. Remove sea objects. To remember where they go, mark each position with masking tape and sketch the particular sea object on it.

Untape the curtain from the floor and remove to your sewing machine. Straight stitch or zigzag stitch the overlays in place. Couch the yarn and metallic thread. Ease top tension to avoid puckering. If necessary, back with paper to keep the fabric from shifting. Remove carefully. In Figure 8-10, some shells are cut from sheer fabrics, appliquéd then stitched with free motion embroidery. The loopy line is also free motion embroidery. Machine embroidery looks delightful on sheer fabrics—the light comes through and "floats" it. The strip of lace midway on the curtain simulates a line of foam at water's edge. Stitched waves at the top toss farther out to sea.

Figure 8-10. Backlit seashell curtain (60″ × 60″).

The simplest way to secure the sea objects is to overlay them with strips of clear plastic or sheer fabric cut to the shapes of the other overlays. Or enclose them in pockets. Since plastic is stiff, use it only if the curtain will be stretched taut. Some purchased shells come with holes that can be threaded through. You can hand-sew these to the curtain. You can also drill holes in shells (more successfully on some than on others) with a jeweler's drill or, if shells are delicate enough, probe holes through

with a needle, then rotate the needle to make a smooth opening.

Keep checking as you add sea objects to see if their combined weight causes the fabric to pull downward. Hang the curtain every once in a while to see if it is being distorted.

Sheer appliqués lead a double life. At night, the lamplight captures the subtleties of the surface decoration, and, by day, the light, coming from behind, silhouettes the shapes and the lively scene.

PADDED SHAPES

To enrich certain areas of the design, shapes are sometimes padded before being stitched in place. Cut the shape larger than the design calls for to allow for stuffing takeup. Place some polyester fiberfill on the background fabric. Place the shape over the background and secure it with straight stitch or narrow zig-zag. Trim edges and any excess stuffing. Finish the edges with a row of satin stitch. Another way is to stitch the shape down first, leave an opening, and then add stuffing. Stuff very lightly to prevent any puckering of background fabric.

Figure 8-12. Detail of orchids by Ellen Toby Holmes. Appliquéd shapes outlined with satin stitch. Velvet background. (Courtesy, The Detroit Gallery of Contemporary Crafts)

PADDED SHAPE

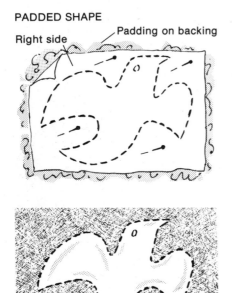

Figure 8-11. Position cutout shape on stuffing and backing, stitch in place. Trim away excess to complete padded shape.

Figure 8-13. Appliquéd circles outlined with blindhem stitch. On other shapes, hems are turned and straight-stitched.

RANDOM APPLIQUÉ

Some appliqués have the charm of a watercolor, with the design defined by lines of stitches overlaying color areas. Such treatment lends a subtle shading to the colors and a light touch to the whole composition. (See Figure 8-14)

To achieve this quality, first make a sketch for the stitch lines, then fill in areas of color to represent the fabric patches. Or pin the patches to the background fabric, overlay them with tracing paper, and then sketch the stitch lines. You can stitch through the paper, removing it carefully when you are finished. Or use the sketch as a guide, and "eyeball" the design as you stitch.

Any stitch or technique can be used to complete your piece. You may need a hoop, especially if you plan to use a wide assortment of stitches, some of which may pucker the fabric.

Figure 8-14. Example of random appliqué. Design defined by stitches; fabric shapes freely cut.

Figure 8-15. Detail of banner, *Climbing Stairs* by Norman LaLiberté (9' × 4'). Satin stitch appliqué. (Courtesy, Arras Gallery Ltd., New York)

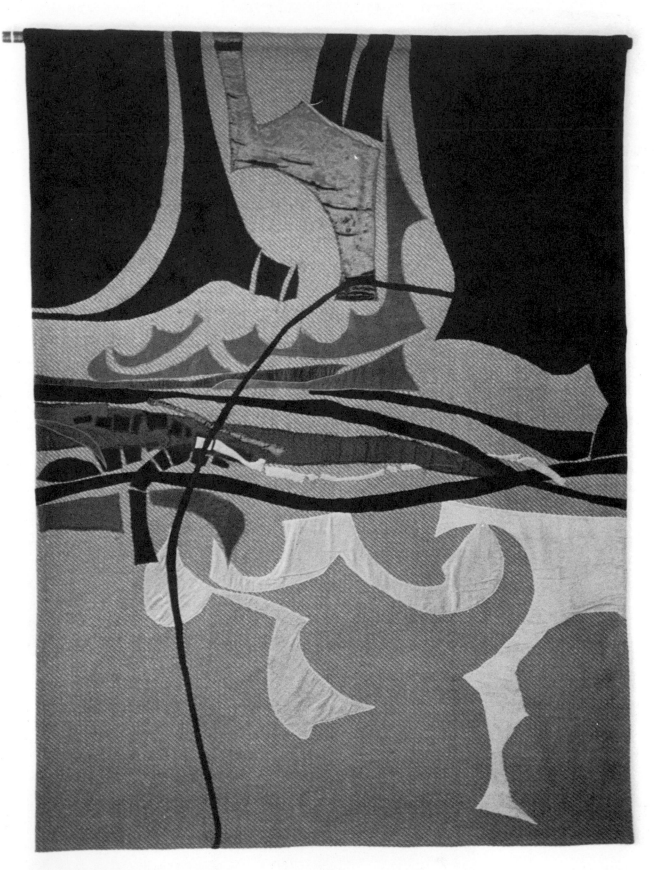

Figure 8-16. Wall hanging by Carolyn Hall
(80″ × 54″). "Painting" with appliqué.
Variety of shapes arranged on upholstery
fabric and appliquéd with satin stitch.

LARGE APPLIQUÉ

Appliqué can also resemble paintings in the placement of shapes and in the harmony and color of the overall design. To achieve this effect in a large appliqué, first lay the background fabric on the floor and fix its position with masking tape. Or lay it on a large table that you can tape to. While the design is in progress, stand away every so often to see it in perspective. For more distant viewing, stand on a chair or stepladder. (You have probably viewed paintings from close up and then from farther away, and discovered how remarkably they changed with distance; the overall design becomes more apparent than the details.) If this arrangement is not satisfactory, pin all the pieces in place and tape or nail the appliqué to a wall. Or pin a wide hem at the top (you will probably need one anyway), run a dowel or drapery rod through, and hang it from a window molding or a door. The ideal arrangement is to alternately move the piece from floor to wall while designing. In that way, you achieve the right sense of balance by walking around the piece when it lays flat and can appreciate the pictorial effect when it hangs vertically.

For best results, choose a firm fabric for the background. Upholstery fabrics are particularly sturdy since most have rubberized or other stiff backings. To firm other fabrics, add a lining or back with paper. If necessary, reinforce shapes with iron-on interfacing.

Measure and mark hems on the background fabric and pin them under, or pin on whatever edging you might be planning to use. Overall size is an integral part of the design; it affects placement of shapes as well as distribution of color.

Make a sketch of your design, or cut out fabric shapes and place them at random on the background fabric. If you would rather not experiment by cutting fabric shapes and perhaps wasting fabric, cut shapes from construction paper or from magazines. These can then become the cutting patterns for the final shapes. Rearrange the cutouts on the background until you find a design that pleases you. Then begin to think in terms of color and texture, and select your fabrics accordingly. When all is settled to your satisfaction, secure the shapes firmly in place with straight pins, safety pins, or with hand-basted stitches.

Roll the piece, leaving a small area exposed for stitching. A large piece can be particularly cumbersome; rolling it makes for easier stitching.

Begin at the closest edge and work in. If you are using safety pins to secure the shapes, remove each pin before you reach it, and replace it with a straight pin.

Outline the shapes with satin stitch, or with a more open zigzag for a less visible outline but quicker results, or with any stitch appropriate to your design.

Figure 8-17. *Old Fashioned Lady* by Margaret Cusack. Appliquéd collage.

REVERSE APPLIQUÉ

Reverse appliqué is a sophisticated method of design created by the San Blas Cuna Indians of Panama. The design is formed by stitching several layers of fabric together and cutting through them to reveal the layers below. Because the machine-sewn stitches press the fabric flat, you do not get the variations in levels, formed by narrow hems and hidden stitches, that are characteristic of the hand-sewn San Blas molas. Still, the technique presented here produces effective results.

Sampler

Refer to Figures 8-18 to 8-23 while making this sampler. You will need three layers of fabric, each 14 by 14 inches (35.6 by 35.6cm), in different colors or patterns; add seam allowances. Use fabrics that do not fray easily.

Make the design on tracing paper, using a compass. First, draw a border around the design area. Then, with

Figure 8-19. Reverse appliqué. Drawing pinned to fabric layers. Darkened areas indicate where first layer will be cut away to reveal second and third layers.

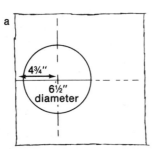

Add 1″ to all sides for seam allowances

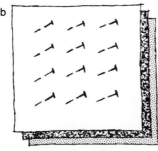

Pin pattern to 3 layers prior to stitching

Figure 8-18. Starting a reverse appliqué design. (a) Paper pattern. (b) Pinned layers.

the compass, draw a circle 6½ inches (16.5cm) in diameter (see Figure 8-18, a). Bisect the circle with a second circle. Place the compass point where the first and second circles bisect, and make a third circle. Make a fourth circle by placing the compass where the second and third circles bisect. Continue in this manner to complete the design.

Since the design will be cut out of the fabric rather than laid on, decide which fabric is to be the most prominent and make that one the top layer; the next preferred will be the middle layer, and so on. Indicate on your drawing where the colors will appear in the final piece. For a completed sketch see Figure 8-19.

Stack the three layers and place the design on top. Pin liberally through paper and fabric to hold them firmly in place (Figure 8-18, b). Set the machine for straight stitch—15 to 20 stitches per inch

(2.5cm), or shortest setting—or for narrow zigzag, and stitch over every line that will appear in the final design.

With small, sharp scissors or clippers, begin trimming away the paper and the fabric layers to reveal the desired pattern. Cut close to the stitching. For the closest cut, hold scissors as shown in Figure 8-21, with the left blade against the stitch line. Where the top fabric is to remain as part of the design, trim the paper away carefully to avoid pulling stitches out. To reveal the second color, trim away paper, then poke the tip of the scissors very gingerly through the top layer and begin cut-

Figure 8-20. Straight-stitching design lines through paper and fabric layers. Narrow zigzag can also be used.

Figure 8-21. Second layer being cut from section (top layer left partly uncut for this example). Note left blade positioned against stitch line for precise cut.

Figure 8-22. Cutting and trimming completed. Note that satin stitch covers an edge and extends over it to hold fabric down.

ting it away. Clip loose threads. Cutting down to the third layer will leave tiny threads hanging out and will look somewhat discouraging, but press on.

When all the excess fabric has been cut away to reveal the design, set the machine for wide satin stitch (4 width was used in the sampler). Test the setting first on the edge of the fabric sandwich or on similar fabric. Back the design with typing paper to keep it stable while being stitched. Stitch over the design lines, placing the satin stitch to extend over the raw edge and onto the fabric. This will hold the fabric firmly in place. If your fabric frays, go over the stitching a second time, using a wider setting.

The sampler can be completed as a pillow cover, a small wall hanging, or a place mat, just to mention a few possibilities.

Figure 8-23. Completed sampler. Satin stitch lines cross to create a rhythmic effect of interlocking curves.

9. QUILTING

Most people associate quilting with making a patchwork quilt large enough to fit a bed, but quilting is actually a sewing technique. In its most basic form, it means making a fabric sandwich—two layers of fabric with filling between—then sewing it together with quilting stitches. The quilting stitches (which can be any stitch—straight, zigzag, etc.) not only fasten the layers together, but also form a pattern. In most cases, they also compress the outlines of patterns, causing the pattern areas to stand out in puffy relief.

Although classical quilting is considered a handcraft, quilts have also been made by machine for as long as machines have been available to home stitchers. Machine quilting, borrowing its inspiration from the past, has contributed its own qualities of precision, strength, and speed. Quilting goes so much faster by machine. Projects that could take weeks, even months, to sew by hand can be completed in days by machine. It goes without saying that hand and machine quilting can be used together in the same piece, just as they have been for years.

Quilting falls into several distinct categories and can be used to make any number of projects, including wall hangings, pillows, blankets, jackets, skirts, purses, toys, sleeping bags, ski clothes, and, of course, quilts.

STANDARD QUILTING

Also known as English quilting, this method is the oldest and most common form of quilting and is the one with the fabric sandwich. Making a small sampler will give you the opportunity to experiment with this technique. Even if the stitches are uneven at first, and the pattern does not turn out the way you expected, little fabric is lost and much experience is gained. Many stitchers, however, like to use everything they make, and, if you are one of those, you can turn the sampler into a pillow face, or a purse front, or a pot holder. Just use better material than you would for the sampler alone.

Figures 9-1. (*Below*) Quilted wall hanging. Design worked in an overall pattern. (Courtesy, Marilyn Leon)

Figure 9-2. (*Right*) Detail of Figure 9-1.

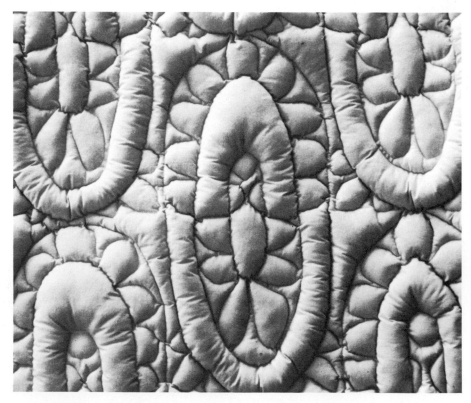

Figure 9-3. Quilted design sampler.
(Courtesy, Marilyn Leon)

Figure 9-4. Quilted design sampler.
(Courtesy, Marilyn Leon)

Sampler

You will need two 12-inch (30.5 cm) squares of sheeting or other closely woven fabric for front and back (choose whites or pastels so stitches will show clearly; save patterned fabrics for later experiments); polyester batting, a single layer 12 inches (30.5cm) square, or polyester fiberfill.

For the design, try a geometric pattern, one with long continuous lines, since these are the easiest to sew on the machine. As you gain experience, you can alter the direction of the lines and add shapes. Work out a design on paper using a pencil, ruler, compass, and French curve. No need to suggest that you be original; twenty people, all trying to do the same flower, would just naturally do it twenty different ways. When you find a design that pleases you and that would be interesting to

Figure 9-5. Quilted purse by Shirley Givens (approximately 12″ × 12″). *(Left)* Front and back unassembled, design stitched on reverse side through paper and fabric sandwich. *(Right)* Finished purse, with trapunto-stuffed areas.

quilt, transfer it to the fabric (see Transferring).

Sandwich the filling layer between the two fabric squares, wrong sides of fabric next to filling. Pin or baste through all three layers to prevent them from slipping as they go through the machine. Set the machine for straight stitch; use a straight stitch foot or zipper foot. Adjust tension to suit the stitching and ease pressure on the presser foot. Stitch carefully over the lines of your design, keeping the layers flat. If the layers shift, pin more liberally in the center of the design as well as at the edges.

For a neat ending to the stitch line, pull on the bobbin thread and bring the top thread through to the back. Knot and clip the ends. Finish by sewing fabric binding tape on the raw edges to cover them; or stitch to other squares, if you are making a series; or finish as suits your project.

After some practice, you will learn how to hold and guide the material so it will be less apt to shift as it goes through the machine. If you cannot decrease presser foot pressure sufficiently, use a darning foot; or work without a presser foot and use your hands to hold the fabric against the needle plate.

Most likely, your sampler turned out well and gave you many ideas for bigger projects. But even if your quilting curled (and you probably struggled to make it lay flat), you have learned something: layered fabrics will curl if they shift in sewing. You can incorporate this principle when you want to make a shaped quilted object. An example of this method can be seen in *Temple Guardian* (Figure 9-7). The curl in the tongue, for example, was built by cutting the top fabric shorter than the bottom fabric, pinning eased gathers into the bottom fabric, then pinning both fabrics together to fit. (When stitching, make sure there are no puckers in the bottom fabric.)

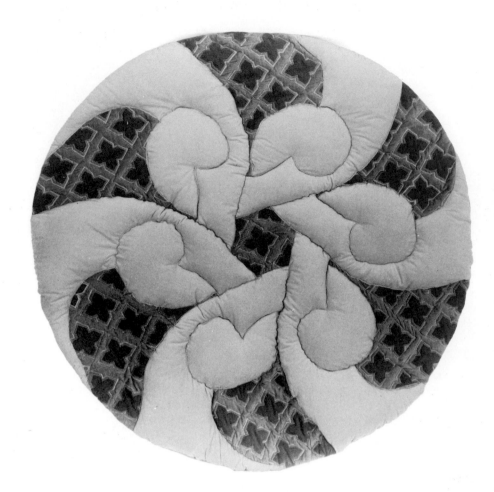

Figure 9-6. Wall hanging by Robin Muller (45″ in diameter). Corduroy and velveteen. Pattern influenced by building embellishments found in the Fan district, Richmond, Virginia. Primary motif similar to one found on a doorknob; background pattern from a cutglass window. Both appliquéd then quilted.

Figure 9-7. *Temple Guardian* by Midori Ishikawa. Quilted wall hanging.

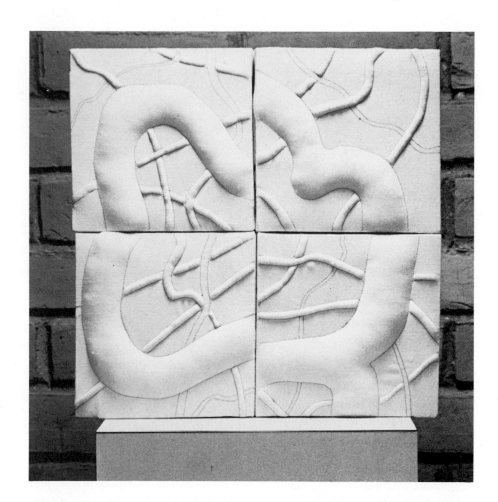

Figure 9-8. *Four Boxes* by Claudia Hall (each box 6″ × 6″ × 4″). Stitched unbleached muslin stretched on box frames, then trapunto-stuffed.

Figure 9-9. Because of similarity of patterns, a number of design arrangements are possible.

TRAPUNTO

This method, also known as stuffed or padded quilting, is used to emphasize certain areas of a design. The areas are first outlined with stitches, then stuffed from the back so they stand out in relief on the face side. This method is also used to add stuffing to an already quilted piece. Trapunto, therefore, can be used to sculpt a raised design on a flat surface or add to the dimension of a quilted surface.

Most fabrics are suitable for use as the top fabric. Velvet or satin are particularly effective in the way they catch the light. Solid colors emphasize the trapuntoed shapes more effectively; printed or elaborate surfaces may compete with the stuffed areas. The backing you choose should not be more flexible than the face fabric, or all the fullness will appear on the back side. Use polyester fiberfill for the stuffing. *Note:* If you plan to shape the fabric into a sculptured form, keep in mind that there will be an additional takeup of fabric, and that the upraised shapes may cause wrinkles in adjacent unstuffed areas. Compensate for this by stuffing lightly and using a flexible fabric, such as wool, for the front.

Set the machine for straight stitch, or set it for free motion sewing if you are planning a complex design. If trapunto is being added to quilted areas, ease pressure on the presser foot. Use a zigzag foot, darning foot, or no foot, as needed, when outlining the design. The outlines can be straight stitched, satin stitched, pattern stitched, couched with a decorative thread, or whatever you

wish. You can also stitch another line to emphasize the outline.

Pin front and back fabrics together, wrong sides facing, and stitch together in the desired pattern. When stitching is completed, turn the piece, backing up, and stuff.

In traditional trapunto, an open-weave fabric is used for the back, and its fibers are carefully parted to make a small opening in the area to be stuffed (see Figure 9-12 *A*). Use an awl, small knitting needle, or other sharp-pointed tool. Still using the tool, push small amounts of stuffing at a time into the opening. Stuff the area to the desired fullness, then work the fibers back into place. Stuff any additional areas in the same manner.

Slit Trapunto. In this method, slits are cut in the backing fabric and are hand-stitched closed after the area is stuffed. Since the sewn slits give a wounded look to the back of the piece, you may wish to sew on an additional backing for a neater appearance. Almost any fabric can

be used for either backing.

Set the machine and stitch a pattern in the same manner as before. Then, with the backing face up, cut a small opening in the center of each area you want stuffed (see Figure *9-12, B).* Select a wad of stuffing, keeping it loose rather than in a ball, and push it into place with a long tool, such as a knitting needle, or ¼ inch (.6cm) dowel sharpened in a pencil sharpener. Adjust the stuffing with the tip of the tool. Or use a strong, sharp-pointed sewing needle to poke through the fabric and move the stuffing about so that no one area is over-padded. The stuffing can be packed firmly for a solid look or packed loosely for a more natural result. When all the areas are stuffed, hand-sew the openings closed with a whip stitch. Surface embellishments may be added, or the face fabric pieced, appliquéd, dyed, or otherwise enlivened. Whether these are worked before or after the piece is stuffed will depend on the individual piece and technique.

Figure 9-10. *Trapunto Basket* a wall plaque by Verda Elliott (approximately 10″ × 11½″). Combines trapunto and basketry techniques; some rows wrapped with yarn.

Figure 9-11. Wall hanging by Sandra Hansen (75″ × 36″ × 3/6″). Trapunto technique with cotton fabric.

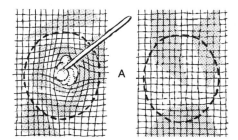

Figure 9-12. Trapunto methods. (*A*) Separate fibers, insert stuffing. Push fibers back in place. (*B*) Slit back, insert stuffing. Stitch opening closed.

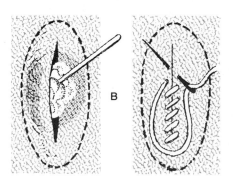

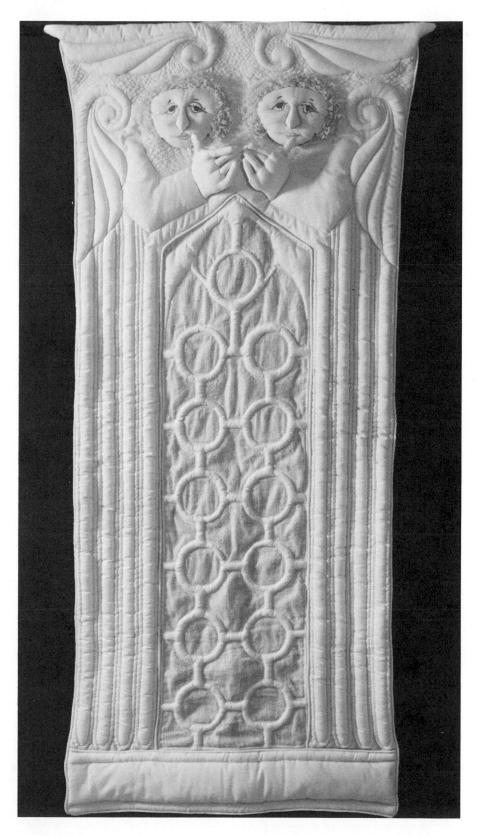

Figure 9-13. *Angel Window* by Elizabeth S. Gurrier (35″ × 60″). Quilted hanging in unbleached muslin and cheesecloth. Trapunto technique *(center area)* with hand-embroidered detailing in faces.

CORDED QUILTING

This method, also known as Italian quilting, is particularly suitable when raised linear patterns are desired on the fabric surface. Corded quilting designs are based on parallel lines, which are stitched then threaded through with yarn.

Select any fabric for the front and a loose weave for the back; not too loose, however, or the pattern will not stand out in relief. You will also need wool or acrylic yarn and a large tapestry needle (this type of needle has a blunt point that pokes its way between the fibers without piercing them). Set the machine for straight stitch.

Plan a linear design in parallel lines, and draw it onto the backing. The lines should form channels wide enough for the yarn to be threaded through—¼ or ⅜ inch (.6 or .10cm). Pin front and back fabrics together, wrong sides facing, and stitch the lines of the design.

When all the lines of the design have been stitched, thread the tapestry needle with one or two strands of yarn, doubling the yarn so that you will be working with two or four strands at a time.

Turn the piece so that the backing faces up. Insert the needle into one end of a channel, and thread the yarn through for a few inches, being careful not to catch the top fabric or go through it. Bring the needle out (see Figure 9-14) and reinsert it in the same hole it emerged from. Continue threading through the channel in this manner.

At sharp curves, bring the needle out, then, if you can, reinsert it in the same hole. Push the needle through as much of the curved channel as possible in order to draw the yarn around the curve. If the needle will not go back into the same hole, clip the yarn, and reinsert it so that the

new end overlaps the clipped end. Do the same at sharp corners or when channels cross.

To end a channel, bring the needle out and pull the fabric, stretching each portion of the design to ease the yarn so that the fabric will not pucker. Then clip the yarn even with the backing. If the design does not stand out enough, thread additional yarn through the channel.

In an alternate method, the entire technique is done by sewing machine.

Twin needles are used and a backing is not necessary. Channel width is dictated by the twin needles, which are spaced ⅛ inch (.3cm) apart. Draw a linear design on the face of the fabric, then, with cord or heavy yarn on the underside, stitch the design onto the fabric face. Use a cording foot or pin tucking foot. Either foot will catch the cord and hold it in the channel. If the design does not puff up enough, you may need to tighten the top tension.

Figure 9-14. Corded quilting. Thread yarn through stitched channels. Work from the back.

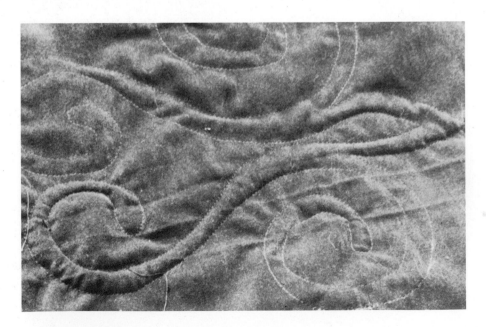

Figure 9-15. Fabric front shows raised result of threaded channels.

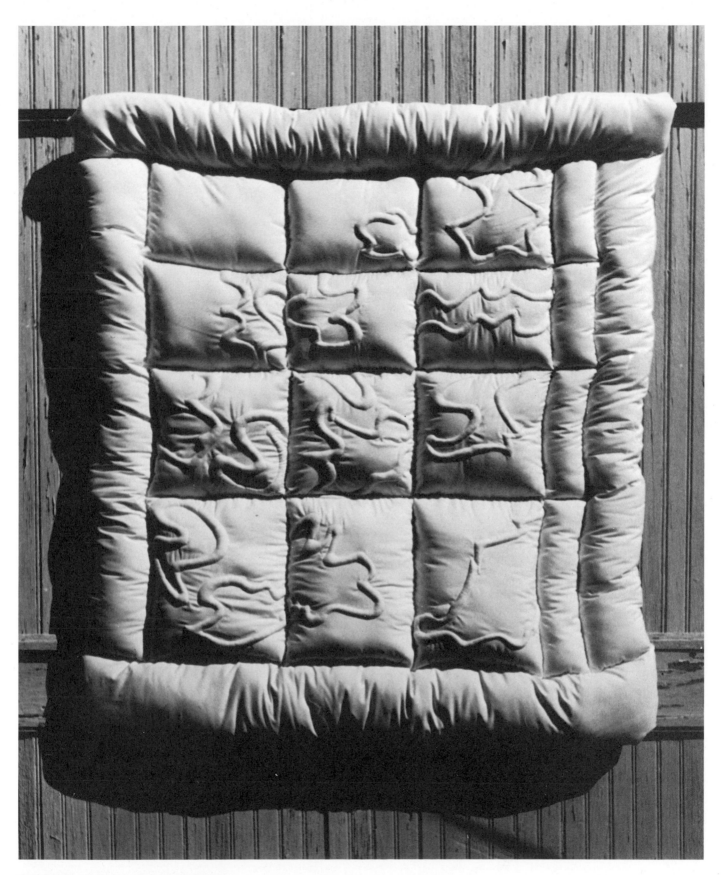

Figure 9-16. *Ho-Ba-La-La* by Joan Lintault
(44" × 40"). Quilted hanging. Wide padded
edge gives effect of frame.

STUFF-AS-YOU-GO

In this technique, individual shapes are stuffed as they are being assembled. They are then stitched together, one after the other, each seam covered by the next seam, resulting in no exposed seams. Every quilt, wall hanging, or whatever piece you make, will present its own challenges and will have to be worked out differently. That is the fun part—devising a plan for each individual piece. The technique for stuff-as-you-go is given in the two projects that follow.

Diagonal Wall Hanging: Project

Finished Size: Approximately 48 by 68 inches (122 by 173cm).

Materials: Velvet, velveteen, corduroy, suede cloth (or your choice)

for the front. See pattern (Figure 9-19) for colors; compute amounts according to measurements on the pattern and in project directions. Your choice of backing fabric, 48 by 68 inches (122 by 173cm). Polyester fiberfill stuffing. 3-inch (7.6cm) binding tape. Dowel or drapery rod. Cord for hanging.

Technique: Set the machine for straight stitch. Use a zigzag or a straight stitch presser foot and ease presser foot pressure; or use a roller foot, easy feed, or a Teflon-coated foot if available.

Directions: Tape the backing to the floor or other flat surface. With a yardstick, draw diagonal lines on the backing as indicated on the pattern (Figure 9-19). Design the entire piece before you begin since it must be made from one end to the other or from the center out to both ends. Lay out the fabrics you have chosen; colors react to one another, and, by laying them out, you will be able to

tell if they all sing together or if one is out of harmony.

Cut all fabric pieces to match the pattern. To obtain measurements for cutting, measure the areas on the pattern then add allowances for seams and fabric takeup. There are three places where seam allowances are added; in the seams that join the pieced sections; in the seams that join the rows; and in the border seams. Allow 1 inch (2.5cm) for these allowances (or less if you prefer). Since each row is stuffed, add extra allowances for fabric takeup. For example, if a row will be 2 inches high, add that amount, or more, to the working width of the fabric (except in the small patches that will be pieced in some rows). If you want some areas higher and some lower, compute each size as you go. Or, easier than computing, fold each fabric to the stuffed shape it will take, then cut it.

After cutting the fabric, follow the pattern and piece the sections for each row. When piecing, turn some patches in alternate directions to give opposing diagonal movement to the nap; the play of light on the fabric will produce an illusion of color change.

When all the fabric is cut and pieced, start at the upper right-hand corner of the pattern and pin the first piece in place. Match its seam lines to the design lines on the fabric. Do not turn seam allowances. Pin lavishly since napped fabrics have a tendency to slide during stitching. Stitch the piece in place along the diagonal seam and along a second side; leave the third side open. Add stuffing, then stitch the third side closed.

Lay the second row, face to face, on the first row so that raw edges and seam lines are aligned; pin in place. Stitch through all three layers—the backing, first and second rows (see Figure 9-18, *B).* Lay stuffing for the second row in place on the backing. Fold the row over the stuffing and stitch it closed on the diagonal seam

Figure 9-17. Diagonal wall hanging (approximately 48″ × 68″)

line (see Figure 9-18, *C),* leaving the ends open for adding or removing stuffing later.

Lay the third row, face to face, on the second row; pin and stitch the diagonal seam in the same manner as before. Lay the stuffing for the third row in place on the backing, fold the row over the stuffing, pin or stitch in place. Repeat for each additional row, stitching each seam to the previous one so that seams are hidden; add stuffing as you go.

When all the rows are stitched in place, adjust stuffing amounts, if necessary, then pin the outside ends closed. Sew fabric binding on all four edges, face to face. Match the top edge of the binding to the fabric edge, stitch on the seam line. Turn the binding to the back of the piece and hand-sew it to the backing. Leave top ends open for insertion of dowel or drapery rod. Attach cords.

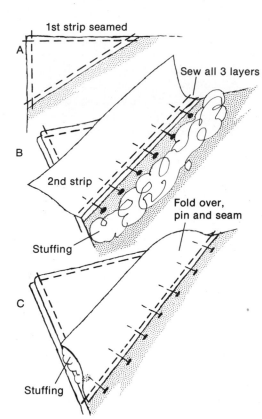

Figure 9-18. (*A*) Stuff first row, stitch sides closed. (*B*) Pin second row to first, seam lines matching; stitch rows to backing. (*C*) Fold second row over stuffing, matching seam line to drawn line on background, and stitch seam. Leave ends open for stuffing adjustments later.

Figure 9-19. Pattern for diagonal wall hanging.

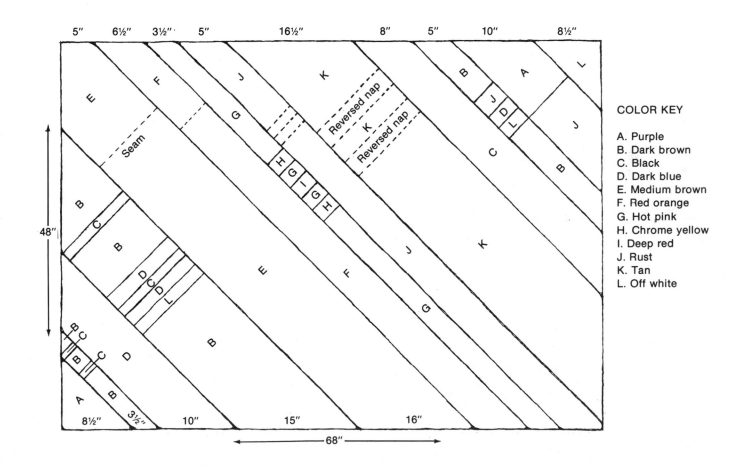

COLOR KEY

A. Purple
B. Dark brown
C. Black
D. Dark blue
E. Medium brown
F. Red orange
G. Hot pink
H. Chrome yellow
I. Deep red
J. Rust
K. Tan
L. Off white

Medallion Wall Hanging: Project

Finished Size: Approximately 81 by 22 inches (205.7 by 55.9cm).

Materials: Soft weave fabrics, preferably wool and wool blends (see following for amounts and colors). Thin sheet of foam (or mattress cover, or quilted lining) for padding. Polyester fiberfill for stuffing. Dowel, 1½ by 14 inches (3.8 by 35.6 cm), and two wooden caps or knobs (finials) for dowel ends. Cord for hanging.

Figure 9-20. Medallion wall hanging (approximately 81″ × 21″). For color, see C-24.

All pieces, except appliquéd circle and square, are joined with 1 inch (2.5cm) seams; circle and square are joined with ½ inch (1.3cm) seams. Seam allowances are included in the dimensions given; allow less if you wish.

Fabric is cut to the following amounts:

Section A: 14 by 26 inches (35.6 by 66cm), white.
Section B: 10 by 26 inches (25.4 by 66cm), black and white checks.
Section C: 24 by 23 inches (61 by 58.4cm), rust; 2 pieces, for front and back. Circle, 13 inches (33cm) in diameter, red.
Section D: 8 by 24 inches (20.3 by 61cm), blue and purple; 2 pieces, (*D1* and *D2*).
Section E: 20 by 20 inches (50.8 by 50.8cm), yellow; 2 pieces, for front and back. Square, 11 by 11 inches (27.9 by 27.9cm), green.
Section F: 17 by 17 inches (43.2 by 43.2cm), pink; 2 pieces, for front and back.

Note: When seams are left open for turning and stuffing, pin or stitch them closed without turning seams under. If stitching, make the stitches within the seam allowance so they will not show when the final seam is sewn shut.

Directions: Set the machine for straight stitch. Scale the pattern (Figure 9-21) and transfer it to the fabric. Cut all fabric pieces. Cut padding to fit section *F* and the large shapes of *C* and *E*. Stitch padding to the backs of these sections to keep them flat. Next, press narrow hems in the 13-inch (33cm) circle and the 11-inch (27.9cm) square. Appliqué in place, following the pattern.

Lay front and back of section *F* face to face and stitch around, leaving the top seam open. Trim corners and seams and turn right side out. Stuff the section, but not too full because you have to stitch through

the layers. Pin or stitch the opening shut (see *Note*). Stitch crossed quilted lines as shown in the pattern, and then proceed with Steps 1 through 9, as shown in Figure 9-22.

Lay *F* on *E*, right sides facing, with the seam line of *F* on the bottom seam line of *E* (Step 1). Stitch together at these seam lines. Keep *F* positioned on *E*.

Section *D* is next. Stitch the two 8 by 24 inch (20.3 by 61cm) pieces together along their widths to make one piece 14 by 24 inches (35.6 by 61cm), with purple as the top color and blue, the bottom. Measure, then cut the joined piece along its length to make three pieces, each 14 by 8 inches (35.6 by 20.3cm) (Step 2). Fold one piece in half, lengthwise edges matching, and stitch along these edges. Trim seams and turn right side out. Repeat for the other two pieces (Step 3). Stuff the three tubes so they are slightly raised. Join them by stitching across the seam line that separates the colors (Step 4); do not join lengthwise seams. Leave the ends open. Lay this section on section *E*, right sides facing. Position and stitch together as shown (Step 5). Keep *D* positioned on *E*. Lay backing over section *E* (with sections *D* and *F* in position), right sides facing. Stitch backing in place, leaving an opening at the bottom for turning. Trim seams and work the pieces through to the right side. Turning may be somewhat cumbersome because of the added bulk. Enlarge the opening if necessary. When the pieces are turned, add stuffing to section *E*, if you want, then turn open seams under and stitch closed by hand or machine.

Next, fold section *A* in half along its length to make a piece 14 by 13 inches (35.6 by 33cm). Stitch the widthwise edges together (Step 6). Turn and stuff; topstitch seams ¾ inches (1.8 cm) in from the widthwise edges to hold stuffing in place. Fold the piece along its width and pin open ends together (Step 7).

Fold section *B* in half along its

length to make a piece 10 by 13 inches (25.4 by 33cm), and stitch lengthwise edges closed. Insert *A* into *B* so that top seams align. Stitch together along those seams (Step 8). Trim seams and corners, turn right side out and stuff section *B*. Stitch a series of bar tacks to make a quilted design and to hold padding in place.

Place joined sections *A* and *B* on section *C*, right sides facing. Stitch together as shown (Step 9) and leave in position. Lay backing over section *C* and stitch around, leaving an opening at the bottom for turning. Trim seams and turn right side out. The hanging is now in two pieces: *A,B,C* and *D,E,F*.

Lay one piece on the other, right sides facing, and the open seams of sections *C* and *D* meeting. Pin and stitch together at these seams, but not through the backing on section *C*. Stitch opening closed by hand or machine. Insert a dowel through the opening in section *A*, and attach cords at both ends for hanging.

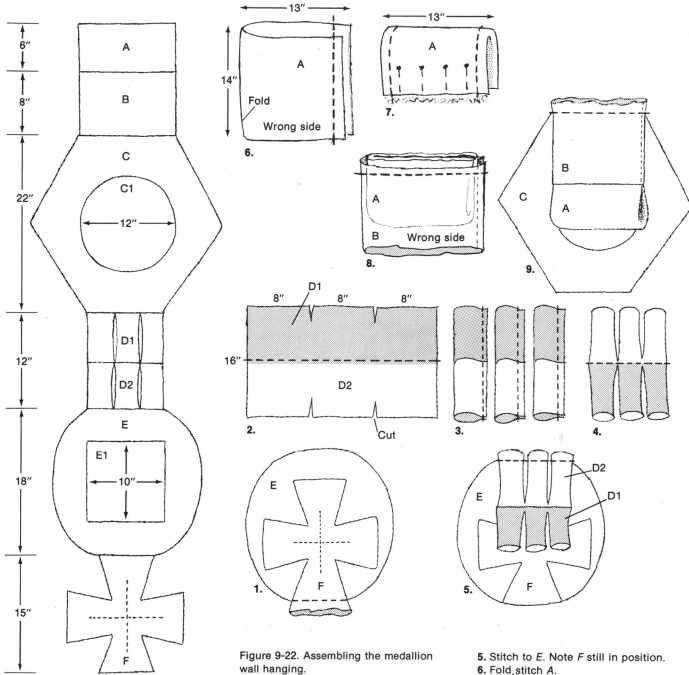

Figure 9-21. Pattern for medallion wall hanging.

Figure 9-22. Assembling the medallion wall hanging.
1. Stitch *F* to *E* at bottom seam.
2. Join *D1* and *D2*, cut into three pieces.
3. Make three tubes.
4. Turn right side out, join across centers.

5. Stitch to *E*. Note *F* still in position.
6. Fold, stitch *A*.
7. Fold in half, pin open ends together.
8. Fold and stitch *B*. Insert *A*.
9. Stitch at seams, insert dowel through open ends of *A*.

10. TUCKS

By making tucks in the fabric, you can form a variety of layered designs. Different fabrics react in different ways to this treatment. Wool sculpts into soft bas relief, cotton folds into crisp lines, and sheer fabrics assume a dimensional quality when light filters through from behind and outlines the layered areas.

Figure 10-1. Stitch a series of tucks, then one tuck down the center. Press series in opposite direction. Stitch two tucks parallel to center, anchoring series in a twist.

For a good first project, make a series of squares using a number of tuck variations. Tiny tucks, large tucks, reversed tucks, grouped, and crossed tucks can be placed in measured order or at random.

A ½ inch (1.3cm) tuck takes up 1 inch (2.5cm) of fabric, so buy at least half again as much fabric as you think you will need. Decide first on the size of the individual squares then add the allowance for tuck takeup. Wools, heavy fabrics, or those that fray, will use up more fabric than will cotton or other lightweight fabrics. Before stitching down the folds, iron them to judge results. Or, if the fabric is expensive or special, make test tucks on newspaper or typing paper first and then stitch them on the machine. The effect will not be exactly the same as with fabric, but it is a way of conserving fabric if you are concerned.

In the process of making the sampler that follows, you will discover many ways to alter or develop the design by making small variations on a theme.

Sampler

Set the machine for straight stitch. From cotton fabric, cut or tear a long strip, 5 inches (12.7cm) wide. You will be making a series of 5-inch (12.7cm) squares. Tucks will be ¼ inch (.6cm) wide—½ inch (1.3cm) of fabric.

For the first square, measure 1¾ inches (4.4cm) in from the end of the strip, and stitch down the first tuck. Stitch a second tuck ¾ inch (1.9cm) from the first; a third tuck ¾ inch (1.9cm) from the second. After finishing the tucks, measure 5 inches (12.7cm) in from the end, and cut off the square (see Figure 10-2). So that dimensions will be accurate, always cut the squares after the tucks have been made, or at least after they have been ironed and pinned in place.

Next, stitch across the center of the square and at right angles to the tuck stitch lines. This anchors the tucks so they lay in one direction. Then press the tucks to lay in the opposite direction. Stitch a line

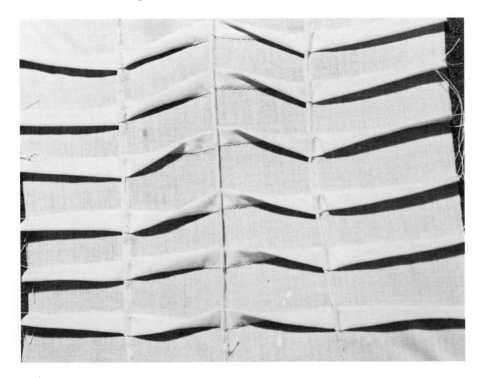

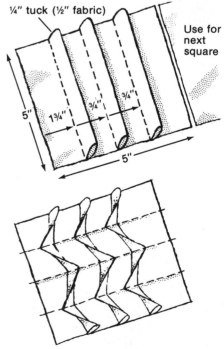

Figure 10-2. Allow sufficient fabric for tuck takeup. Complete each square before cutting it off strip. Stitch tucks in opposite direction to twist them.

¾ inch (1.9cm) from the center line and parallel to it. Stitch another line the same distance away and on the other side of the center line (see Figure 10-2). This anchors the tucks in an upraised twist.

Make additional squares in the fabric strip. Try variations. Sew a number of tiny vertical tucks, spacing them at regular or irregular intervals, and cross them with horizontal stitch lines. Place horizontal lines at the top and bottom of the square so that the tucks twist in opposite directions. Or reverse every other tuck to the back of the fabric for a pleated effect.

A 5 inch (12.7cm) width is sufficient for vertical tucks, but greater variety can be achieved by adding tucks that move horizontally and diagonally. From the fabric, cut or tear a long strip, 7 or 8 inches (17.8 or 20.3cm) wide, and make another series of squares by stitching the

tucks, pressing them in one direction, then crossing them with other tucks (see Figure 10-1). Make wide tucks and narrow tucks. Because of overlapping seams, some areas in a square can be 6 layers thick, so choose your fabric with this in mind.

When you have completed a number of squares in various designs, arrange and then join them into one large square. Trim the seams after joining; or turn raw edges under and stitch them down for a clean finish; or add a lining to the back instead. You can also join the squares and cover their seams with fabric binding tape; make the seams on the right side of the fabric and stitch the binding over them. Do the same with the outside edges.

This technique need not be limited to squares; try other shapes as well. Individual or massed tucks can be used to emphasize details on stuffed forms, or to embellish sections where

Figure 10-3. Tablecloth by Virgina Frantz (43 × 43″). Forty-nine tucked squares, joined together by making seams on right side and covering them with fabric tape.

you have used other techniques. Tucked pieces can be appliquéd or pieced. A variety of shapes can be used to make wall hangings, soft sculpture, screens, drapery, tablecloths, place mats, and other pieces.

11. SOFT SCULPTURE

Most of the techniques and examples to this point have dealt with flat surfaces or with pieces raised in bas relief. In this section, the emphasis shifts to shaped objects and forms.

Patterns for flat or slightly raised pieces are usually fairly easy to figure out but grow more complex as dimension is added. Since some fabric is taken up by the stuffing, shapes need to be drawn "fatter." Therefore, if you cut two pattern pieces for a rounded shape, cut them a little more than one and a half times as wide as the finished object. The shape may seem overly fat, but stuffing and seams will bring it into proper proportion. Fortunately, fab-

rics are flexible, and some are stretchy and can be molded around forms.

If you plan to embellish a shape with other techniques, such as patchwork or appliqué, do so before assembling. Machine embroidery or couching should be done before cutting the shape, since some slight puckering occurs with these techniques. Additional enhancement includes painting or dyeing the shapes, applying lines or designs with felt-tipped pens, and even having children draw their own portraits in crayon.

Figure 11-1. *Five Lady Friends* by Brooke Greeson (6′ × 6′ × 2′). Soft sculptured costumes. Chicken wire armature. The stuffed muslin figures are supported by Ms. Greeson's outstretched arms.

Figure 11-2. Lifesize fabric sculpture by Patricia Maloney (26″ × 20″ × 38″). Built on a welded steel armature. Fabric airbrushed with dyes, paints, and clay. (Courtesy, Kay Moran)

Figure 11-3. *Arial Act* by Lenore Davis (18″ × 18″ × 4″). Direct-dyed cotton velveteen.

Figure 11-4. *Angel Pillow* by Elizabeth S. Gurrier (10″ × 18″ × 4″). Quilted and stuffed unbleached muslin. Machine and hand embroidered. Photographer, Bob Raiche. (Courtesy, Detroit Gallery of Contemporary Crafts)

Unturned Forms. Since these shapes are not turned, their seams will be exposed. To make fairly simple shapes, cut two pieces of fabric for front and back. Firmly woven fabrics that do not ravel easily are best; felt is a good choice. Sketch the shapes freehand or trace them from magazines or other sources, and transfer to the fabric. Simplify shapes if they are complex. Arrange them singly or in groups, as you prefer. Pin front and back together, *wrong* sides facing, and join them with straight or satin stitches. Leave an opening for the stuffing. Stuff, then stitch the opening closed.

Turned Forms. When assembling, pay special attention to corners since these are stress points in turned and tightly stuffed shapes. If possible, avoid stitching too sharp a corner;

Figure 11-5. *Chorus Girls* by Wendy Midiner (10″ × 24″). An example of an unturned form.

Figure 11-6. *(Above)* Armlet. Felt, stitched and stuffed jewelry. *(Below)* Pin. Both by Gail Farris Larsen.

sew inward corners with a little curve (Figure 3-7, *B*). Turn corners and narrow areas completely and neatly by pushing them out gently with the rounded end of a pencil or knitting needle. Make the opening for turning and stuffing on the least conspicuous seam. If a shape has been painted, turn very carefully so as not to mar the surface. If damage does occur, patch the area with matching colors, blending them in with long strokes of the brush.

How to Stuff. Different types of shapes have different stuffing requirements. Some shapes also have armatures, or frameworks, made of wood, wire, or some other firm material. For most shapes, the stuffing is pushed into place with a stuffing tool—a pencil, knitting needle, dowel, or something similar. You can buy dowels in different sizes as needed, and whittle one end or sharpen it with a pencil sharpener. Sandpaper the sides if they are not smooth. The pointed end of a pencil is ideal for poking small bits of stuffing into corners or tiny areas;

be sure the point is blunt, or else the lead may leave marks showing on the outside of the fabric.

Add stuffing a little at a time; large wads ball up and are difficult to smooth into shape. Wrap the stuffing around the pointed or rounded end of a stuffing tool and push it into place. For long, tubular shapes, roll stuffing into finger-size bundles and insert. Do not pack too solidly so as to avoid pulled-out seams, lumps, or distorted figures. You can shift the stuffing about by pushing a sharp needle through from the outside.

Tubular sections are stuffed more easily while they are being turned. To do this, turn the tip of the tube to the right side; push stuffing into place, turn more of the tube, and add more stuffing. Continue in this fashion, and then roll the section between your hands to distribute the stuffing evenly. Be sure these sections will fit through the opening left in the seam.

Some stuffed pieces require that the stuffing be fixed in place. This can be done in various ways: by quilting the layers, by sewing stuffing in place with hidden basting stitches, or by making pockets inside the shape to hold the stuffing. Stuffing can also be wound with string, thread, or fabric to sculpture the shape. Foam stuffing can be carved to shape.

Once a form is stuffed, stitch the opening seam shut by hand or machine. Add any finishing touches, such as buttons, yarn, trim, pieces of fur, or whatever else completes the piece.

Star: Project

A simple turned and stuffed shape.

Materials: Metallic-coated fabric (available at display supply stores, and at fabric stores during holiday seasons), two pieces, each 5 inches (12.7cm) square, for front and back. Polyester fiberfill stuffing.

Technique: Straight stitch or narrow zigzag. Cotton-wrapped polyester thread in the machine.

Directions: First make a pattern for the shape. Using a compass, draw a circle 4½ inches (11.4cm) in diameter. Set a protractor at the center point and divide the circle into five parts, each equalling 72°. Mark each angle and connect marks to make a five-pointed star. Follow the diagram (Figure 11-7), and draw the cutting lines, curving them slightly from ½ inch (1.3cm) at the tips of the star to ¾ inch (1.9cm) at the angles. Seam allowances are included. This makes a plump star.

Pin the two pieces of fabric together, right sides facing, and pin the star pattern over this. Trace around the pattern, or stitch through it. Begin on one side, about ½ inches (1.3cm) from a tip or an angle. Use small stitches at tips and angles, and reinforce these points. Make rounded corners at the tips, slightly rounded curves at the angles. Leave an opening of at least a ½ inch (1.3cm) on one side for turning and stuffing, more if you are using a bulky fabric.

Trim the seams, tapering them as you near the tips. Cut straight across each tip, about 1/16 inches (.16cm) from the stitch line. Clip to the stitch line at the angles.

Turn the star to the right side. With a pointed tool, carefully push the tips out, one at a time. When the star is completely turned, check to see if any seams have pulled out. If so, turn to the wrong side; restitch the seams and then reinforce them with additional stitches.

Stuff the star with polyester fiberfill. Pull out a small tuft of stuffing from its bag, put it onto the end of a pointed tool and push into one of the tips. Insert all the way to the end. Keep adding stuffing, bit by careful bit, until the area bounded by the tip and its two angles is completely filled. Repeat this process for the remaining tips. Lastly, push tufts of stuffing into the center of the star until it is as full as you wish. Turn the opening seam under, and carefully blindstitch it closed by hand.

PATTERN FOR STAR

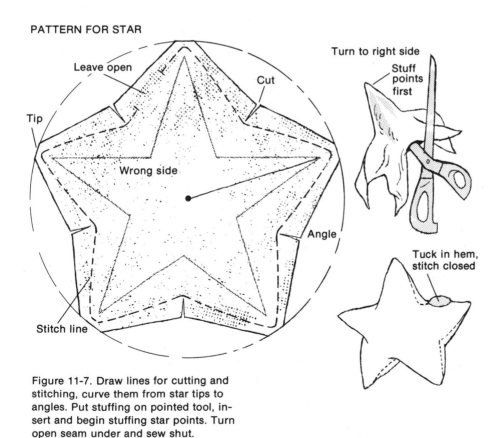

Figure 11-7. Draw lines for cutting and stitching, curve them from star tips to angles. Put stuffing on pointed tool, insert and begin stuffing star points. Turn open seam under and sew shut.

Figure 11-8. Stars. Turned and stuffed metallic-coated fabric.

ROUND SHAPES

Making a ball is a good way to experiment with round shapes. One way to begin is by drawing seam lines on a balloon or plastic ball with an ink marker, then cutting fabric to match. There are many design possibilities: you can make a patchwork design, or a spiraling design, or join two semi-circles with gathers. Another method is to begin with the fabric itself. Gather it around a ball, pin and stitch the folds (see Figure 11-9). Trim away the excess. (Soft, stretchy fabrics are easier to use and require fewer seams than firm fabrics, but the latter maintain the shape better.) The round shapes that follow are cut (without using a ball) and then stuffed.

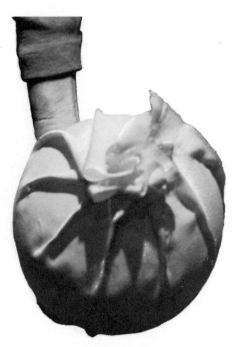

Figure 11-9. One way to make a round shape. Fold and pin fabric around a ball, stitch folds, and trim away extra fabric.

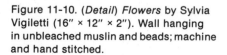

Figure 11-10. (*Detail*) *Flowers* by Sylvia Vigiletti (16″ × 12″ × 2″). Wall hanging in unbleached muslin and beads; machine and hand stitched.

Simple Round Shapes. To make a simple, gathered and stuffed 12½ inch (32cm) ball, cut a 14½-inch (36.8cm) circle (12½ inches plus 1-inch seam allowance all around) out of fabric. Use the longest stitch on your machine (about 6 stitches per inch on most machines) and stitch around the circle, on the seam line. Do not clip thread ends. Stitch a second row in the seam allowance, ¼ inch (.6cm) from the first, and in the same manner. Roll stuffing to make a firm 4 inch (10.2 cm) ball and wrap with string to maintain the shape. Place the ball on the fabric circle. Gather the fabric around the stuffing by drawing up the bobbin threads. Add more stuffing if needed. Draw threads up as tightly as possible. Thread them through a needle and hand-sew the opening shut.

Wedge Shapes. In this ball, wedge-shaped sections are stitched together then turned. For a ball approximately 20 inches (50.8cm) in circumference with eight vertical sections, make a rectanglular template, 10 by 2½ inches (25.4 by 6.6cm). Add ½ inch (1.3cm) seam allowances, for a total of 11 by 3½ inches (27.9 by 8.9cm). Find the center of the rectangle. With the center as a guide, draw a line down the length of the rectangle, another across its width. Connect these lines to make a wedge shape, as shown in Figure 11-11, *A*. Place the fabric face down and trace around the template. Cut out eight sections. Stitch them, one to the other, at their curved sides (see Figure 11-11, *B*). When you reach the last seam, join it at top and bottom only, leaving an opening, as shown. Turn right side out, stuff, and stitch closed. This shape can be loosely stuffed or solidly packed; it will hold its shape either way.

To make this ball in another size, first decide on the circumference (distance around), then on the number of vertical sections. To find the

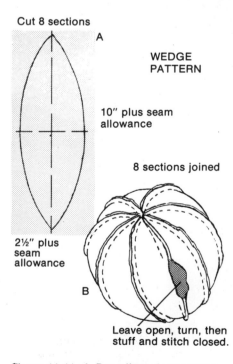

Cut 8 sections

A

WEDGE PATTERN

10″ plus seam allowance

2½″ plus seam allowance

8 sections joined

B

Leave open, turn, then stuff and stitch closed.

Figure 11-11. *A*. Draw lines down center and across width, connect to make wedge shape. *B*. Stitch shapes together.

length of the rectangle for each section, divide the circumference in half. To find the width, divide the circumference by the number of sections. Remember to add seam allowances.

Pentagon Shapes. Still another type of ball is made with pentagons. Decide on the size of the ball, then on the size of each pentagon. Next, make a template for the pentagons. Using a compass, draw a circle; set a protractor at the center point and divide circle into five parts, each equalling 72°. Mark the angles, connect them with straight lines, and cut out the template.

Place fabric face down, trace around template, and cut out twelve pentagons. This ball is made in two sections. Choose one pentagon as the center of the first section and sew five pentagons around it (Figure 11-12, *A*). Repeat for the other section. Fit and stitch the two sections together (Figure 11-12, *B*), leaving one seam open for turning and stuffing. This ball will keep its shape very well.

Interlocking Shapes. Baseballs and tennis balls are made by sewing two bar bell-like shapes together so they interlock. For a ball 8 inches (20.3cm) in circumference, cut two rectangles out of fabric, each 2 by 6¼ inches (5.1 by 15.9cm), plus ½ inch (1.3cm) seam allowances.

Directions are for one rectangle; repeat for other rectangle. Refer to Figure 11-13, *A*. Measure down 1 inch (2.5cm) from the top and 1 inch (2.5cm) in from one end of the rectangle to find its midpoint (of course, do not include seam allowances). Set a compass on that point and draw a 2-inch (5.1cm) circle. Repeat at the other end. Draw a line from one circle to the other, dipping it in ⅛ inch (.3cm) at the halfway point, as shown. Repeat for other side. The width of the shape at the halfway point will be 1¾ inches (4.4cm). Cut out the shapes (include seam allowance).

To assemble, stitch the A's of one piece to the B's of the other piece, then lap the remaining A's around (Figure 11-13, *B*). Leave one seam open for turning and stuffing. This ball needs to be fully stuffed to become round. To make a ball in an-

other size, first decide on the distance around (circumference). Divide the circumference by 4 to find the size of each circle. The width of the rectangle will equal 3 times the size of a circle, plus the amount of dip at the halfway point between two circles.

PATTERN FOR INTERLOCKING SHAPES

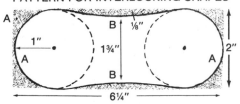

Add seam allowances   Cut 2

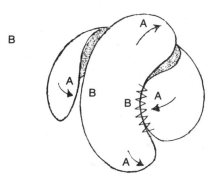

Figure 11-13. (*A*) Follow pattern to make one rectangle. Repeat for second rectangle. (*B*) To assemble, stitch two A's to two B's. Stitch remaining A's in place.

PENTAGON PATTERN

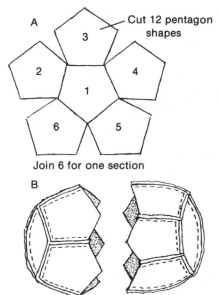

Figure 11-12. (*A*) Join six pentagons to make one half of ball. Repeat for other half. (*B*) Fit and join the two halves.

Figure 11-14. Design variations on a ball by Betty Oros. An experiment in round shapes. The embroidered ball, top center, was purchased.

UPHOLSTERED SHAPES

In this technique the stuffing process is reversed—instead of designing a shape and then stuffing it, you shape the stuffing and then cover it. The stuffing, foam rubber or polyurethane foam, is available in upholstery shops, department stores, and fabric stores, and comes precut in various shapes and thicknesses. However, if you cannot find the shape you want, you can easily cut your own. You can also glue sections of foam together with foam glue (available at upholstery stores) to get the size you want. For example, if

you have a foam form, 30 inches (76.2cm) wide by 72 inches (182.9cm) long, but you want a form, 36 inches (91.4cm) wide by 60 inches (152.4cm) long, you could cut off the extra 12 inches (30.5cm), divide it into two sections, each 6 inches (15.2cm) wide by 30 inches (76.2cm) long, and glue them to one side of the form to get the desired size (see Figure 11-15).

After the foam shapes are cut to suit the design, use them as cutting patterns for the face fabric. Reverse the cutout face sections and use them as cutting patterns for the back. Pin the fabric pieces to the foam shapes to see how they fit. You may discover that you have to ease fullness around outward corners or curves and use less fabric on the inward ones. When assembling, remember to leave an opening for

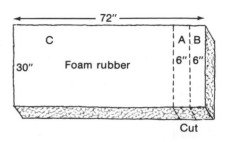

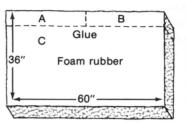

Figure 11-15. To get desired size of foam stuffing from existing size, cut excess from one end and glue to sides.

Figure 11-16. *Space Rings* a toy by Sharon Lynch. This imaginative soft sculpture is designed to be played with. Double-knit fabric over polyurethane foam.

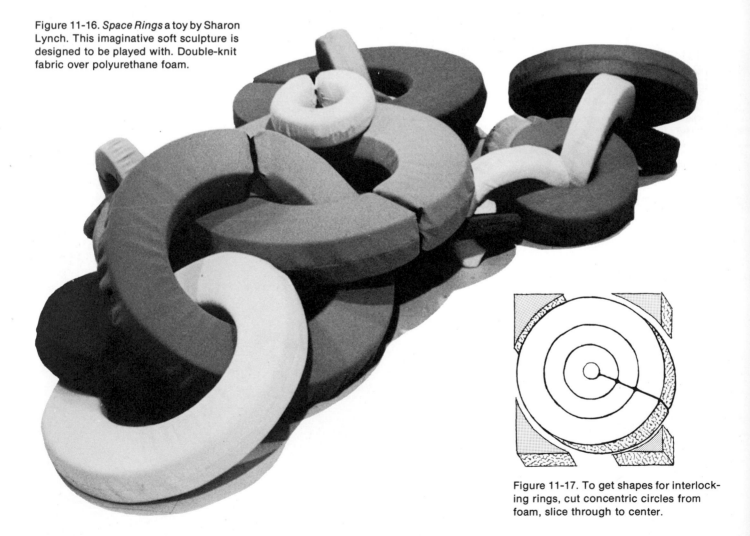

Figure 11-17. To get shapes for interlocking rings, cut concentric circles from foam, slice through to center.

turning and inserting the foam. Hand stitch the opening closed, or fasten with Velcro. If the piece does not fit well, if it pulls on the corners, or wrinkles on the inward curves, rework. Snug-fitting covers look best. Adjustments can also be made in the fit by adding small amounts of stuffing, such as polyester fiberfill, to corners or wherever extra firmness is needed.

Making upholstered shapes that interlock is an interesting use of this technique. Interlocking rings, such as those shown in Figure 11-16, can be made by drawing a series of concentric circles on a foam form, then cutting out the shapes and using them as patterns for the fabric. To interlock the rings, slice each foam shape through to its center (Figure 11-17). If you want a lot of rings, you can cut them out of a foam mattress. Upholstered rings can be used to make large chains, costumes, terrain for small toys, or whatever else strikes your fancy.

U.S. Puzzle (Figure 11-18) is another example of interlocking shapes. The shapes are designed in the same manner as any jigsaw puzzle, that is, with "knobs" and/or "slots" that fit one into the other. Note that the corner pieces have knobs or slots on two sides; edge pieces, on three sides; and center pieces, on four. Press the knobs into the slots for a firm fit.

Designs can be painted on the fabric with dyes, then accented with felt-tipped pens, either before or after the shapes are cut out. The fabric can also be appliquéd or machine embroidered.

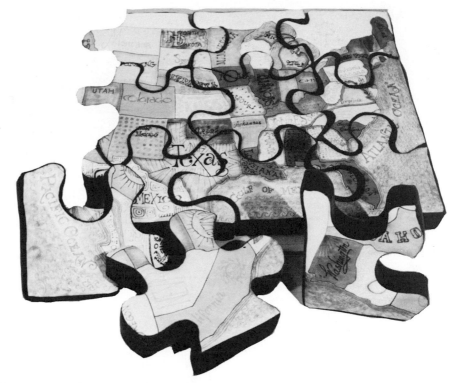

Figure 11-18. *U.S. Puzzle* by Carolyn Hall (36″ × 60″ × 4″). All shapes interlock one into the other. Cotton suede over polyurethane foam. Design painted with dyes and accented with felt-tipped pens.

Figure 11-19. Soft sculpture by Huruno Iwashiro (3′ × 6′ × 18″). Screen-printed design on velveteen.

111

MAKING REALISTIC STUFFED FIGURES

Realistic stuffed figures make delightful companions—a soft fabric cat never meows to go out in the middle of the night; a stuffed macaw never squawks raucously or throws bird seed on the floor. To make your own fabric creation, draw sketches, either from a live model or from photographs, or from books or magazines. While making the sketches, decide how to interpret your subject—serious or sad, funny or quizzical. Certain features can be exaggerated. For example, overly large heads, eyes, and feet can make individuals look childlike. Cartoon figures are often greatly exaggerated. These exaggerations add up to style.

Choose fabric that suits the subject. Napped fabrics were used for the macaw (Figure 11-20) because their richness and depth of color seemed suited to bird's feathers. Determine where the pattern pieces should be joined; seams that appear in unnatural places destroy the illusion of reality. In the macaw, color is the key to unobstrusive seams; each adjoining piece is a different color. Seams also provide the most logical places for shaping. If the figure is all one color, or does not divide easily by color, then, except for the side seams, make as few seams as possible and make them along center lines. Alternately, you may decide to stitch a multitude of seams to add character to the figure and to provide shaping.

Realistic figures are supported from within by an armature of wire or dowels. The armature represents the bone structure of the figure, and the stuffing, tied to the armature, represents the muscles.

Macaw: Demonstration

The first step in making a realistic figure is to draw three full-sized views: back, front, and side. Since I did not have a live model, I drew my sketches from a book. The macaw in this demonstration is on a perch, but it could stand on its feet as well.

Stand: This consists of a round wooden base, a long pole, and a dowel (for the perch). The base and perch are attached to each end of the pole with screws; two bolt holes are drilled in the perch where the armature will be affixed.

Armature: Two metal coat hangers, bent to shape, make an adequate armature for the 24 inch (61cm) macaw; a larger figure, made with heavier materials, would require thicker wire. The wires for the feet are bent with pliers or by hand, then looped around the bolts and twisted so that they are firmly anchored (Figure 11-21).

Figure 11-20. Stuffed macaw. 24" tall. For color, see C-20.

Figure 11-21. Wire armature bent to shape, secured with bolts.

For a free-standing figure, omit the stand and shape the supporting wires for the feet to prevent the figure from tipping over. Study your sketch and determine how the armature should be shaped to give the best support. Draw the lines on your sketch, then bend the wires to this shape.

Padding: For the body, form polyester fiberfill or cotton batting into a bundle and tie to the armature with string (Figure 11-22). Build up the shape by adding stuffing in small amounts. For flat sections, such as the wings and tail, cut foam rubber sheets to shape, following your sketch, and pin in place (Figure 11-23). Measure across the entire side and back views of the sketch to obtain the total width of these sections. The padded form acts as a dressmaker's model for fitting the pattern; the finished shape will be more solidly packed. As you do each step, check with your drawing for measurements.

Fabric: The 24 inch (61cm) macaw requires approximately 1 yard (91cm) of napped fabrics in the following colors: black, white, gray, yellow, and blue.

Face: Trace one side of the face from your sketch to make a pattern for both sides. Include decorative lines and add seam allowances. Transfer the tracing to white fabric and cut out the shapes. Satin-stitch the lines with black thread. Each eye is a flat yellow button, painted black in the center; but a flat yellow button and a round black one would do as well. Pin the eyes in place. Pin the face sections onto each side of the model to see the effect. Developing a pattern requires constant trying on. Sometimes you may have to discard what you have done and start again. If you want to make a permanent pattern, transfer the shape of each fabric section to muslin or paper as you go along; mark seam

allowances and note any adjustments.

Beak: Trace one side of the upper beak to make a pattern for both sides. Transfer to black fabric and cut out the shapes. (Or, measure the sketch and draw the shape directly onto the fabric with chalk, Figure 11-24). Place together, wrong sides facing, and stitch around, leaving an opening at the top for turning and stuffing. Repeat for lower beak. Trim the seams, then sew the two beak sections together. After turning and stuffing, compare with the sketch. If the shapes need redoing, remove stuffing and stitching, and start over again. When you are satisfied with the shapes, remove the stuffing and turn to the wrong side to make an accurate tracing for your permanent pattern.

Neck/Upper Breast: Measure one side of the neck/upper breast on your sketch to make a pattern for both sides. Cut these out of black fabric. Pin one neck/breast section to one face section. Since both shapes curve where they meet, the easiest way to join them is to position the black fabric over the white fabric, right sides facing up, and pin together. Topstitch near the edge to appliqué in place. Satin stitch over the raw edge of the black fabric, using black thread (see Figure 11-25). Repeat for the other side.

Crown: Measure the width and length of the crown on your sketch, and cut the shape out of blue fabric. Machine-baste along the front of the crown and halfway down each side. Draw up the threads to gather the fabric. Fit onto the model and adjust gathering. Indicate the gathers on your permanent pattern. Next, measure the section at the base of the beak (between beak and crown) and cut one piece out of gray fabric. Run basting stitches along its bottom edge and draw up to gather. Stitch to the top of the beak.

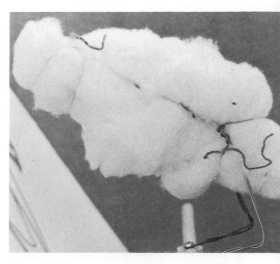

Figure 11-22. Stuffing tied with string and shaped to represent muscles.

Figure 11-23. Thin sheets of foam rubber for wings and tail.

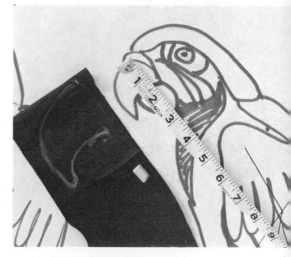

Figure 11-24. Measuring upper beak, drawing shape on fabric.

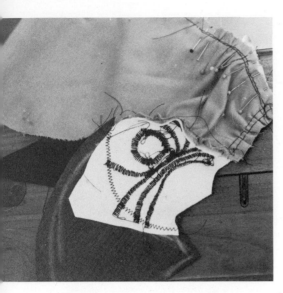

Figure 11-25. Head pieces stitched in place, first one side, then the other.

Figure 11-26. Fabric and paper patterns pinned to model. Note completed head.

Figure 11-27. Body pieces pinned in place.

Assembling Head: Pin one gathered side of the crown to one side of a face section, right sides facing. Place pins ¼ inch (.6cm) or less apart and distribute the gathers evenly. Stitch in place. Next, pin the assembled beak to crown and face. Join with stitches (Figure 11-25). Repeat for the other side. Stitch the breast seam part way down the center. Turn and stuff the completed head. Fit onto the model. Do not be discouraged if you have spent a lot of time and only have managed to finish the head. Since heads require detailing and accuracy, they are almost always the most time-consuming part of a figure.

Body: Measure the back and cut the shape out of dark blue fabric. Measure the tail and cut it out of light blue fabric. Pin both in place (Figure 11-26). Remove the foam sheets for the wings while you work on the body. For the underbody (and for all large shapes) make a paper pattern first. Measure the area and cut the paper to size. Measure the distance between the legs and cut leg holes in the paper. Cut paper patterns to go around the upper legs. Pin paper to the model. Trim, fold, and shape wherever necessary. Mark the paper where joinings occur. Remove paper and cut the shapes out of yellow fabric.

Stitch back and tail sections together where they meet. Pin all fabric sections to the model (Figure 11-27). Fabric drapes differently than paper and stretches as well, so adjustments in the body and legs will probably be necessary.

Assembling Body: Unbolt the model from the stand and remove the fabric, leaving as many pins in place as possible. Next, remove the pins from the right side and repin all the seams on the inside. This will take some time and skill. Stitch the pieces together, leaving an opening under one wing for turning and stuffing.

Tail: Fold the tail around the foam padding and pin the seam at the end.

From yellow fabric, cut a long, tapered piece for the underside of the tail. Pin it to the outer tail. Remove foam, turn tail pieces wrong sides out, and repin. Stitch the bottom seam of the outer tail, then stitch the underside in place (Figure 11-28). Stuff the foam back into the tail—it should be a snug fit.

Stitch up and down the tail to simulate feathers and to hold the stuffing in place (Figure 11-29). Then stitch the body to the tail. The only body seam remaining open is the one for turning and stuffing.

Feet: For the lower legs (the upper legs have already been stitched to the body), cut two pieces of gray fabric, fold each leg section, right sides facing, and stitch its side seam. Turn and slide each one onto armature. For the feet (toes), cut eight narrow pieces of gray fabric, and stitch them to shape (Figure 11-30). Then trim and turn to the right side with the aid of a crochet hook. Cut thin wires to twice the length of each toe. For each toe, wrap stuffing around the wire and insert, pushing stuffing all the way to the end. Keep wire in place so that half extends outside (the wire allows toes to be bent to any shape). Push more stuffing in with a long tool. Make two bundles of four toes each, and twist the wires firmly around the top of each bundle.

Wings: To allow for additional shaping, the wings are divided into two sections: wing and wingtip. Separate the foam sections, first marking them so they can be joined again at the same angles. For one wingtip, cut two pieces of blue fabric. Seam together, wrong sides facing, turn, and carefully insert foam. Topstitch to simulate feathers and to hold foam in place. Repeat for the other wingtip. For the two upper wings, cut two pieces of light blue fabric. Run basting stitches around their edges and draw up to gather the fabric. Insert foam. Pin upper wings to wingtips. Satin stitch a scalloped design on the upper wing to simulate feathers and to join the wing sections (Figure 11-31).

Completed Macaw: Fit the shape onto the armature. With a long tool, push wads of stuffing carefully in place through the open seam; pack firmly. Handsew the seam closed. Pin the wings in place and handsew with hidden stitches around the upper wings. Sew the eyes tightly in place. Bolt the bird to the perch and tighten the bolts. Arrange the toes so that they cover the bolts, and wrap them realistically around the perch (Figure 11-32). Twist the excess wire (from the toes) tightly around the armature wire to hold toes in place. To finish, you have only to pull the fabric of the lower legs over the wires and handsew them to the tops of the toe bundles.

If you are making a permanent pattern, check the pattern pieces to make sure that all seam allowances, directions, and necessary changes have been noted.

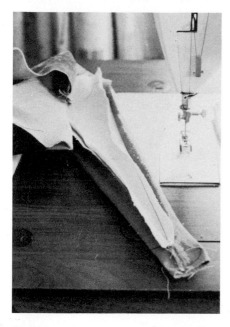

Figure 11-28. Tail pieces being stitched together. Foam removed.

Figure 11-29. Tail stitched to simulate feathers.

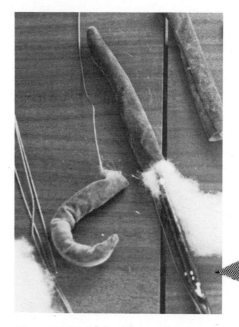

Figure 11-30. Method for making toes.

Figure 11-31. Before final assembly. Note scalloped design on upper wing.

Figure 11-32. Completed macaw and original sketch.

115

PAINTED SHAPES

Applying paints or dyes to fabric is yet another way to achieve well-defined details, delicate shading, and distinctive design. Painted shapes, such as those shown in Figures 11-33 to 11-35, can be made by applying acrylic paints to firmly stuffed surfaces. Acrylic paint (available in jars and tubes at art supply stores) is thick and opaque and comes in a rainbow of colors. It is soluble in water and becomes permanent when dry. Use finely woven fabrics such as muslin, cotton, or linen as background for the paint—the fabric acts as the canvas.

Draw the outline of a shape on the fabric. Since design emphasis will be on the painted surface, the shape can be quite simple. Stitch the shape together, right sides facing, using the finest stitch on your machine to keep fabric from fraying. Trim, turn, and stuff firmly. Hand-sew the opening closed. If the shape will be on a base, insert an armature before closing the open seam; stiff wire or dowels can be used for small

Figure 11-33. *Singing Group* by Dee Durkee. Painted stuffed shapes on armature.

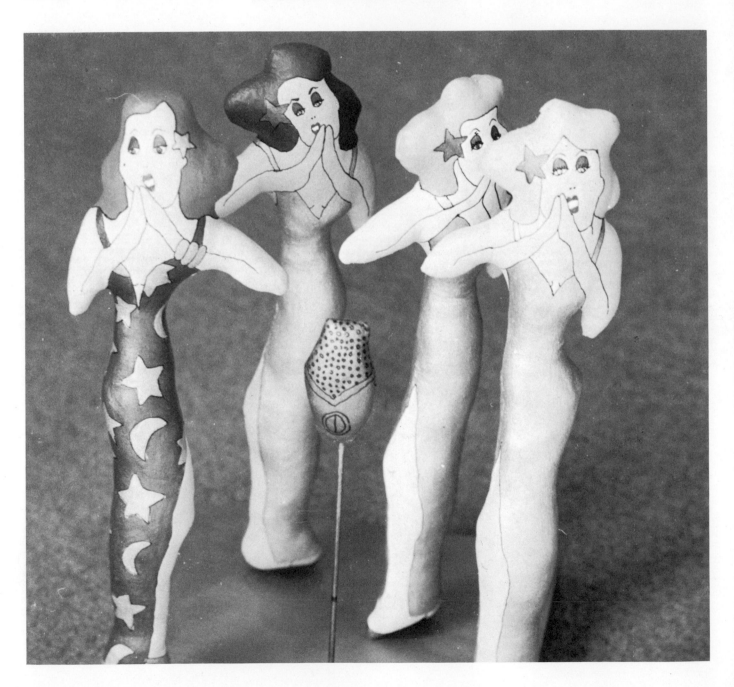

figures. Drill a hole in the base to hold the armature.

To prepare the fabric, apply an undercoating of white acrylic paint. Use a paint brush and allow paint to dry completely before applying another coat. Several coats may be needed to obtain a smooth ground for the design. Thin with water for best results; if applied too thickly, the paint will crack or peel off. Once the surface is prepared, begin painting your design, allowing each color to dry completely before applying another near or over it. For a more flexible surface, omit the undercoating, and brush or stipple the paint directly on the fabric.

Depending on the design and the desired effect, paint can be applied to stuffed shapes or other projects before or after they are assembled. In addition to the acrylic paint, you can also use latex paint, acrylic house-paint, textile paint, and dyes. Textile paints and dyes do not require an undercoating. Dyes painted on wet fabric with a watercolor brush achieve a soft shading; subsequent coats intensify the colors and define design areas. Dyes are available in dime stores, craft shops, or through dye-houses. The numerous ways to dye fabrics, each a separate craft, could take several volumes to cover thoroughly. For further information consult craft books on tie-dye, batik, screen printing, and other dyeing techniques.

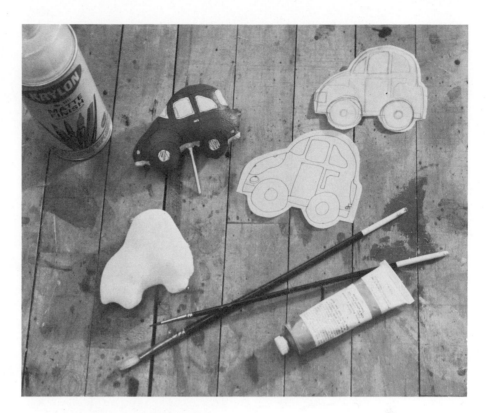

Figure 11-34. Painted stuffed car from drawing to completion, by Dee Durkee.

Figure 11-35. Stuffed and painted shapes. Lapel pins by Dee Durkee.

Figure 11-36. *Woman with Hat Looking
Up* and *Woman with Hat Looking Ahead*
by Lenore Davis (both 27½" tall). Direct-
dyed cotton velveteen.

Figure 11-37. *(Left) Two-Faced Woman* by Mary Jane Mazuchowski. Batik-dyed cotton fabric. Machine-sewn and stuffed. *(Right)* Figure on other side of form.

' Figure 11-38. *Standing Sisters* by Susan
K. Andrews (16″ × 11″ × 4″). Stuffed
shapes; richly embroidered and decorated. Painted features, appliquéd
flowers; use of quilting, including
trapunto.

120

Figure 11-39. *Fred and Ginger Dancing* by Susan K. Andrews (12″ × 18″ × 4″). Painted and stuffed shapes. Combined machine techniques of appliqué, embroidery, and quilting, including trapunto.

Figure 11-40. Stuffed figure by Dale Schumacher (19″ tall).

INDEX

Page numbers in italics refer to illustrations.